W9-ACH-369

EXPLOSIVE POWER

Also by **Health For Life:**

- **Legendary Abs II**

- **Beyond Legendary Abs**
  A synergistic performance guide to Legendary Abs II and SynerAbs

- **Power ForeArms!**

- **T.N.T.—Total Neck & Traps**

- **Maximum Calves**

- **The Human Fuel Handbook**
  Nutrition for Peak Athletic Performance

- **The Health For Life Training Advisor**

- **SynerStretch:** For Whole Body Flexibility

- **Minimizing Reflex and Reaction Time**

- **Amino Acids and other Ergogenic Aids**

- **Secrets of Advanced Bodybuilders**
  A manual of synergistic weight training for the whole body

- **Secrets of Advanced Bodybuilders:** *Supplement #1*

ISBN 0-944831-28-1
Library of Congress Catalog Card Number: 93-79689

Health For Life
8033 Sunset Blvd., Suite 483 — Los Angeles, CA 90046 — (310) 306-0777

1 2 3 4 5 6 7 8 9

EXPLOSIVE POWER

Plyometrics for Bodybuilders, Martial Artists & other Athletes

by Ed Derse

Health For Life

To my mother who taught me to jump far *and*
my father who taught me to jump high.

CREDITS AND ACKNOWLEDGMENTS

Special thanks to
Donald Babbitt, Eric Boyles,
Mark Hoffman, Robert Miller,
Jerry Robinson,
Brian Shiers, Skip Stolley,
John Tansley and
Wayne Wilson for their
guidance and suggestions
in the development of
Explosive Power

Edited by Robert Miller
and Jerry Robinson
Book design and
illustration by
Irene DiConti McKinniss
Typesetting by Jack Hazelton

CONTENTS

PART ONE — Foundation

PART TWO — Training

An Important Note To All Our Readers...

Plyometrics is a controversial subject among exercise scientists. Some charge that plyometric training is too intense to be beneficial—that it almost guarantees injury. We feel this is a little like saying that racing cars shouldn't be allowed to burn high-octane gasoline because it's too flammable.

*The issue is not the value of the tool, but its appropriateness for your training goals and physical condition. Plyometrics **is** a high-performance technique, intended for the serious athlete, and should never be undertaken carelessly. In particular, lower-body plyometric exercises are not for the overweight or for athletes with existing knee injuries. But for those willing to proceed with appropriate caution, **Explosive Power** offers a concise, sound program guaranteed to deliver optimum results.*

PART ONE

Foundation

PLYO-*what?*

This book is about explosive power—the ability to generate as much force as possible *as quickly as possible.* Explosive power stands apart as the single most important component of athletic performance. This book is also about certain physical adaptations that occur along the way as you train for explosive power—changes that benefit bodybuilders in the pursuit of greater muscle mass. The key to both results is a specialized form of training called **plyometric training.**

So what is plyometric training, anyway? The word *plyometric* roughly means to increase or augment. Russian and European coaches developed the plyometric technique in the late 1960s, but it's still relatively unfamiliar to most Americans. Strictly speaking, you don't do plyometrics—you do certain exercises *plyometrically.* Actually, most of us have done some form of plyometric exercise at some point in our lives. Remember jumping rope, playing hopscotch, leaping from the front porch, and skipping across the front lawn? All of these have plyometric qualities.

Plyometric training capitalizes on certain predictable responses that occur when you subject a muscle to a sudden overload. It works like this....

Say you're holding out your hands, expecting to be handed a silk necktie. Instead, someone drops a watermelon onto them from five feet up. The sudden weight overloads your biceps, causing them to stretch. Almost instantaneously, the lengthening biceps contract powerfully to prevent you from dropping the watermelon.

This type of contraction—one that occurs while a muscle is being stretched suddenly—happens as a result of an unconscious reflex. Central to plyometric training's effectiveness is the fact that this reflex can generate much greater force than any consciously motivated contraction. By repeatedly subjecting a muscle to sudden overloads, you increase its *eccentric strength* and improve its ability to convert that strength into explosive movement.

This approach differs tremendously from conventional strength work—the vast majority of which involves the maximizing of voluntary contraction. While conventional weightlifting, in particular, has the dual advantage of being able to isolate individual muscle groups *and* being less physically strenuous than plyometrics, it is insufficient as a means of developing maximum athletic power. To develop the speed-strength required in martial arts, track-and-field, and other sports, plyometric training reigns supreme.

Equally exciting, though, is the advantage plyometric training offers to bodybuilders. **Explosive Power** will explain how bodybuilders can use the plyometric technique to achieve strength and size gains not attainable through conventional weight training alone!

Onward now to some basic information you need to know before you can begin using plyometrics—starting with the answer to what sounds like a simple question but, in fact, isn't...

How strong are you?

❖   ❖   ❖

STRENGTH, POWER, & SPEED-STRENGTH

Ask an Olympic weightlifter, a bodybuilder, a martial artist and a volleyball player what strength is and you'll get different answers. The Olympic weightlifter and bodybuilder are likely to respond in terms of their "maxes" for a particular lift. The martial artist will probably say something about breaking boards, or punching or kicking power. And the volleyball player will talk about the ultimate spike.

In fact, each of these athletes—and each sport—depends on several different kinds of strength. In preparation for exploring the role strength plays in **Explosive Power** training, let's take a look at athletic strength in its various forms. We'll also cover some other important athletic qualities that are often thought to be types of strength, but aren't—**power** and **power-endurance**.

ABSOLUTE STRENGTH

The fundamental measure of muscle performance is **absolute strength**. Absolute strength refers to the **total contractile capacity** of a muscle—that is, the total tension that would result were all a muscle's fibers to fire in response to maximum stimulation by the nervous system. You can't bring absolute strength to bear in "real world" situations because your central nervous system won't let you. This built-in defense mechanism prevents you from injuring your musculo-skeletal system. It also makes it virtually impossible to measure total contractile capacity voluntarily.

Maximum strength is the most common measure of muscle performance. This is the kind of strength bodybuilders and powerlifters are referring to when they talk about their maxes. Your maximum strength is the greatest amount of force you can generate voluntarily, and is always less than your absolute strength (Fig. 1).

MAXIMUM STRENGTH

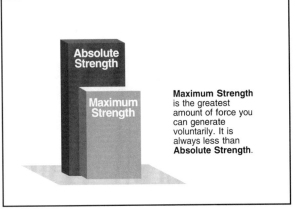

Fig. 1 — Absolute Strength vs. Maximum Strength

Maximum strength varies depending on the type of muscle contraction involved. So to explore maximum strength fully, we have to take a closer look at the nature of muscle contractions.

There are three types of muscle contractions: **concentric**, **isometric**, and **eccentric**. Each is characterized by what happens to the *length* of the muscle during contraction.

During a *concentric* contraction, a muscle shortens and its corresponding joint angle changes. This is what most people picture when they hear the words *muscle contraction*. The first half of a standard dumbbell curl involves a concentric contraction (Fig. 2a, next page).

Types of Muscle Contractions

Concentric Contractions

5

Isometric Contractions

During an *isometric* contraction, both muscle length and joint angle remain the same. Picture standing in a door frame pushing out against the jamb with each arm. Your deltoids are definitely contracting, but they neither shorten nor lengthen, and the angles at your shoulders don't change. An isometric contraction also occurs at the bottom of the curl as you change direction from going down to going up (Fig. 2b).

Eccentric Contractions

During an *eccentric* contraction, the muscle *lengthens* as it contracts because the associated joint angle widens. This can happen because the load is too great for the muscle to overcome or because you voluntarily limit the intensity of the contraction. Our watermelon example in the introduction involved an eccentric contraction. So does the second half of that dumbbell curl (Fig. 2c)—the biceps are still contracting, but the biceps lengthen and the weight lowers because you voluntarily limit the intensity of the biceps contraction.

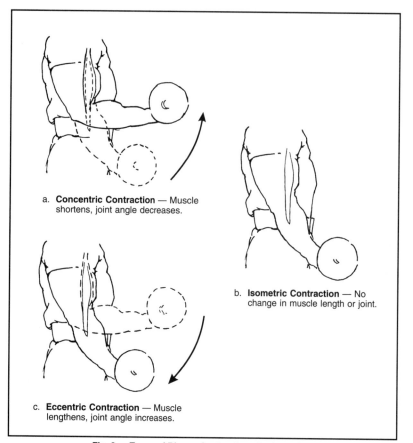

a. **Concentric Contraction** — Muscle shortens, joint angle decreases.

b. **Isometric Contraction** — No change in muscle length or joint.

c. **Eccentric Contraction** — Muscle lengthens, joint angle increases.

Fig. 2 — Types of Biceps Contractions During a Curl

Corresponding to these three types of muscle contractions, you have concentric, isometric, and eccentric measures of maximum strength.

Your concentric maximum tends to be the lowest of the three but it's the most easily determined. You just find the most you can curl, bench press, squat, or whatever for one rep and that's your concentric max for that lift.*

Concentric, Isometric, & Eccentric Maximums

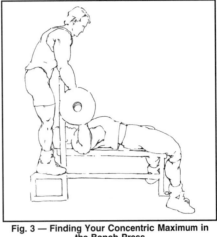

Fig. 3 — Finding Your Concentric Maximum in the Bench Press

Your isometric maximum is usually pretty close to your concentric maximum, but it depends a lot on the joint angle at which you take the measurement. You might think you could find your isometric max for a particular lift by increasing the weight until you reach the amount you can't budge. For reasons we won't go into here, the results produced by this technique are inaccurate. Measuring the isometric max safely and accurately requires a device called a *tensiometer*.

Of the three types of contractions, eccentric muscle contractions are the strongest. In fact, your *eccentric* maximum tends to be about 40% to 50% greater than your *concentric* maximum, very nearly approximating your absolute strength.

One way to determine your eccentric maximum for a particular bodypart is to increase the eccentric load to the point of fail-

*Before trying to determine your concentric max for any lift, be sure to read the safety precautions in *Appendix A*.

ure during an exercise for that bodypart. To do this, you increase the amount of weight until you can't lower the barbell, dumbbell, or cable handle under control. You should use extreme caution when doing this, as you can be severely injured if you do it improperly. **For safety's sake, please read the more detailed instructions in *Appendix A* before trying this technique.**

Voluntary Activation Capacity & Strength Deficit

Once you know your eccentric and concentric maximums, you can calculate a much more useful value called your **voluntary activation capacity**. This is the part of your absolute strength you can actually use.*

To find your voluntary activation capacity, you express your concentric max as a percentage of your eccentric max. For instance, if your concentric max for a knee extension is 150 lbs and your eccentric max is 200 lbs, this shows that you can voluntarily lift (150 lbs. ÷ 200 lbs) × 100%, or 75% of your absolute maximum—a voluntary activation capacity, then, of 75%.

The difference between voluntary capacity and absolute capacity is called your **strength deficit**. In the example above, the strength deficit would be 25%.

The size of the strength deficit reveals a lot about the nature of your strength. Top athletes usually have very small strength deficits for most muscles—just 5% to 10%, implying a highly

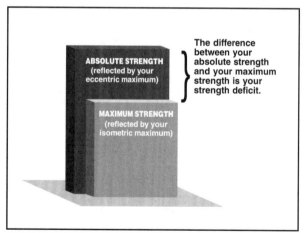

Fig. 4 — Strength Deficit

---

*The most accurate way to calculate voluntary activation capacity involves your *eccentric* max and your *isometric* max. But because finding your isometric max involves special equipment, and given that your concentric max is nearly the same as your isometric max, we are going to substitute concentric max for isometric max in our calculations.

developed activation capacity. Lesser athletes show deficits as high as 45% to 50%.

The size of your strength deficits suggests the type of training you need to do. Although this is much simplified, athletes with very low strength deficits need to train for hypertrophy, or an increase in overall muscle mass. Those with large strength deficits need to train to increase maximum strength. Knowing your strength deficits is crucial to productive training.

While voluntary activation capacity affects all athletes, it has a special meaning for bodybuilders.

Bodybuilders often reach plateaus where they experience severe decreases in their gains from training. When this happens, they usually *increase* training volume—an approach that may result in overuse syndrome, injury, and loss of hard-earned muscle mass. (Not to mention leading them down the path to training gimmicks and steroid use.)

Several factors can produce plateaus—one is large strength deficits. That's because, although the way most bodybuilders train packs on tremendous muscle mass, imparting impressive absolute strength, it doesn't necessarily produce great maximum strength.

With a big gap between maximum strength and absolute strength, even all those extra sets and reps may not represent enough of an overload to stimulate continued growth.

If you are a bodybuilder reaching a point of diminishing returns, determine your strength deficits for the major muscle groups. They're likely to be larger than the 5% to 10% that

Bodybuilding & the Strength Deficit

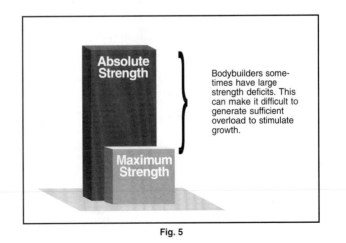

Bodybuilders sometimes have large strength deficits. This can make it difficult to generate sufficient overload to stimulate growth.

Fig. 5

characterize those of most top performance athletes. If that's the case, you need to put the goal of hypertrophy aside for a while and focus on raising your voluntary activation capacity. That's what **Explosive Power** is all about. Once you have increased your voluntary activation capacity, more traditional weight training will once again produce a sufficient overload to stimulate additional mass gains.

SPEED-STRENGTH

While measures of absolute and maximum strength tell how "strong" you are, they don't say much about how well you *use* that strength. In fact, research shows that absolute strength alone is a relatively poor predictor of performance. Many powerlifters with impressive maximum strength are actually outperformed by weaker athletes when required to lift a much lighter weight for speed. Since most sports require movements using body weight or implements much lighter than a loaded barbell, powerlifters are often relatively unathletic in the use of their strength.

This points up the fact that, in most sports, effective use of strength requires figuring in another variable—*time*. It's not enough to be able to apply force. You have to be able to apply force *quickly*. This ability is sometimes misnamed "athletic strength." It's properly called **power, explosiveness,** or more commonly these days, **speed-strength.**

Once again, speed-strength is a measure of strength in relation to time. It describes how long it takes you to produce the maximum amount of force you can generate.

Speed-strength is vital in sports. Imagine two basketball players of equal size. One can generate 600 lbs of leg force in 3 seconds. The other can produce 500 lbs of leg force in 2 seconds. Who has the better functional power? The second player.

He or she produces roughly 250 lbs of force per second (500 lbs ÷ 2 sec.), whereas the first player produces only 200 lbs per second (600 lbs ÷ 3 sec.). In any sport dominated by fast movements, the athlete who can use strength more quickly has the edge.

Components of Speed-Strength

Speed-strength has two components: **starting strength** and **explosive strength.** *Starting strength* is the measure of your ability to generate force—of any amount—at the start of an action. *Explosive strength* is the measure of your ability to reach *maximum* force output in the least time. Both elements affect athletic performance.

Starting strength is the fundamental type of strength required by any sport involving quick movement without much added resistance. Sprinting, jumping, and throwing light implements all demand good starting strength. Each individual movement in these activities happens in the fraction of a second where starting strength comes into play.

Starting Strength

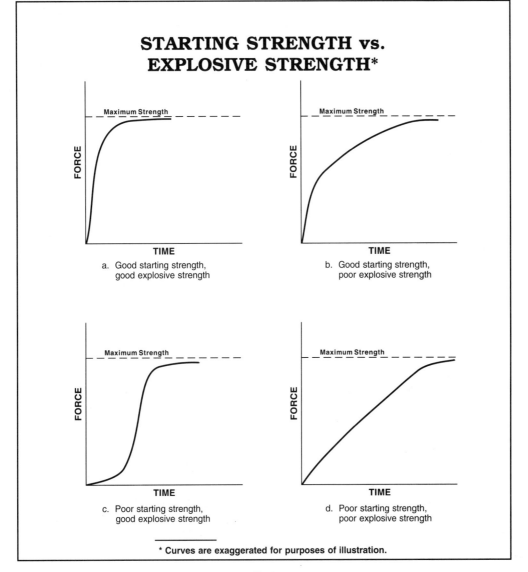

STARTING STRENGTH vs. EXPLOSIVE STRENGTH*

a. Good starting strength, good explosive strength

b. Good starting strength, poor explosive strength

c. Poor starting strength, good explosive strength

d. Poor starting strength, poor explosive strength

* Curves are exaggerated for purposes of illustration.

Fig. 6

Explosive Strength

Explosive strength, on the other hand, is the ability to bring maximum force to bear quickly. If you have good explosive strength, you will be more successful in activities that require effort against resistance. Weightlifters and football players, for example, rely heavily on explosive strength.

Interestingly, even though both starting strength and explosive strength are components of speed-strength, an individual who has good starting strength may not have good explosive strength, and vice versa. In fact, even some relatively weak people have fairly good starting strength because they can use what little strength they have quickly.

The distinction between starting and explosive strength becomes important when constructing your training. You need to develop both to maximize explosive power and also to realize your full athletic potential.

POWER-ENDURANCE

The final measure of athletic strength is **power-endurance.** Like power, *power-endurance* involves a time element, so technically it isn't a form of strength at all.

Power endurance is the ability to muster maximum, or near maximum, power repeatedly over time. Optimum performance in most sports requires this ability. Martial artists, boxers, basketball players, volleyball players, wrestlers, Olympic lifters and, in fact, most athletes need to be powerful over the entire course of competition. Martial artists and boxers certainly want to hit or kick with force near the end of a bout as well as the start. A basketball player or volleyball player needs those few extra inches of jumping ability near the end of the game. Often, it's that little extra bit of power that separates the champion from the also-ran!

Regardless of your sport, true athletic strength is a lot more than a measure of the amount of weight you can bench press or squat. While your max is certainly a good measure of basic strength, it says very little about how well you can use your strength. To use basic strength effectively in sports, you must convert it into explosive power.

To do that, you must develop strength and speed together...and *that* is the purpose of the **Explosive Power** plyometric program detailed in the chapters that follow.

MEASURES OF STRENGTH

	DEFINITION	APPROXIMATED BY
Absolute Strength	The **total contractile capacity** of a muscle	Eccentric Maximum
Maximum Strength	The greatest amount of force you can generate voluntarily	Concentric Maximum
Voluntary Activation Capacity	The part of your absolute strength you can actually use	(Concentric Maximum ÷ Eccentric Maximum) × 100%

MEASURES OF POWER

	DEFINITION
Speed-Strength	Strength in relation to time. Speed-strength describes how long it takes you to produce the maximum amount of force you can generate.
Power-Endurance	The ability to muster maximum, or near maximum, power repeatedly over time.

❖   ❖   ❖

THE PHYSIOLOGY OF PLYOMETRIC TRAINING

NEURO-MUSCULAR CONDITIONING

The Stretch Reflex

As we've said, the effectiveness of plyometric exercise comes from the conditioning that takes place when a muscle is forced to resist a sudden load—conditioning that affects both **neurological mechanisms** and the **natural elastic properties** of muscle.

This chapter deals in more detail with the adaptations that occur in both areas. In doing so, it sets the stage for turning plyometric *concepts* into plyometric *training*.

We'll start by focusing on the main neurological mechanism behind the plyometric technique, one we referred to right at the outset—**the stretch reflex**.

The stretch reflex originates deep inside each muscle fiber with a structure called the **muscle spindle.** The muscle spindle is a complex construction of muscle protein, fluid, and nervous system receptors. Within this structure is a special type of muscle fiber that does not have the contractile qualities normally associated with muscle. These special fibers, called **intrafusal fibers,** are wrapped with nerve cells that relay information from muscle to the central nervous system. When a muscle is stretched quickly, the tension in the intrafusal fibers stimulates these nerve cells, sending messages out to the cen-

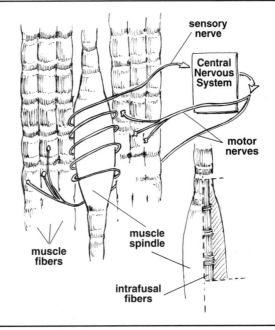

Fig. 7 — Muscle Spindles and Intrafusal Fibers

tral nervous system at great speed. In response, the central nervous system triggers a muscle reflex that generates a fast and powerful contraction (Fig. 7). This reflex is the **myotatic, or stretch, reflex.**

The stretch reflex is a protective mechanism that provides an extra burst of strength to resist force encountered suddenly.

Imagine stumbling over a curb while crossing the street. As your momentum propels all your weight onto your forward leg, the sensory fibers in your leg muscles send a message to the central nervous system, which in turn triggers the stretch reflex. The reflex results in a fast and powerful contraction of the leg muscles, preventing your fall.

But the stretch reflex is more than just a protective mechanism. It is also integral to peak performance. Sprinting at full speed involves a series of eccentric contractions enhanced by multiple stretch reflexes. The power generated by these contractions helps propel you forward at full speed.

The stretch reflex is the physiological foundation of plyometric training. When the reflex is triggered, a very large proportion of the muscle's fibers suddenly contract. The resulting very powerful eccentric contraction is much stronger and faster than a consciously initiated concentric contraction—because it involves a greater percentage of absolute strength.

By taking advantage of the stretch reflex to generate powerful eccentric contractions, plyometric training allows you to train more of your muscle capacity than you can using the simple concentric contractions typical of conventional weight training. And by increasing utilization capacity (the difference between absolute and maximum strength), you train more efficiently, become athletically stronger and pave the way to increased usable strength and muscle mass gains.

Maximizing Stretch Reflex Intensity

The intensity of the stretch reflex is a consequence of how fast and far a muscle is stretched. For training to be truly plyometric, the preliminary loading, or stretching, of the muscle must be done quickly. This is a fundamental principle of plyometric training: **The *rate of stretch* of the muscle is more important than the *degree of stretch*.**

When the muscle is stretched slowly (within a normal range of motion), it does not sense any immediate threat of injury, so the stretch reflex is not triggered. To take advantage of the body's reflexive power, the stretch must happen quickly.

Suppose you are doing the plyometric exercise known as Two-Leg Power Hops (Fig. 8). To achieve the proper effect, you must jump, land and rebound with as little time spent on the ground as possible. Compare this to jumping, landing and

Fig. 8 — Two-Leg Power Hops

sinking into a full squat before attempting the rebound hop. When you slow the motion, the stretch reflex mechanism is minimized and the exercise loses its plyometric effect. Again, the *rate* of stretch, not the amount, makes the difference.

The stretch reflex is the primary feature of the neuro-muscular system involved in plyometrics. But there are two other important neuro-muscular aspects of athletic performance developed by plyometric training as well.

ADDITIONAL NEURO-MUSCULAR CONDITIONING

Eccentric to Concentric

The first is the ability of a muscle to switch quickly from an eccentric (lengthening) contraction to a concentric (shortening) contraction. This ability depends in good part on the absolute strength of the muscle. But it also depends on how efficiently the neuro-muscular system can make the transition from eccentric to concentric movement. Plyometric training develops the neural patterns involved in this transition. As a muscle becomes familiar with the demands of sudden overload, it "learns" to fire more fibers with greater speed. When a muscle is able to recruit more of its fibers at a greater speed, the transition time from eccentric to concentric contraction decreases.

This ability to switch quickly from eccentric to concentric is especially important for athletic performance. Most single actions in sports take place in tenths of a second. In the 100-meter sprint, for example, each footfall stays on the ground roughly one-tenth of a second. When a basketball player goes to dunk a ball, the jump foot remains on the ground for roughly two-tenths of a second. In both cases, all the force of the action must be applied in a fraction of a second.

Traditional strength training techniques—such as concentric weight training—cannot address this specific demand. In a typical conscious muscle contraction, it takes six to eight tenths of a second to achieve peak muscle force. Clearly, this type of strength training fails to meet the fundamental criteria of specificity.

But plyometric training produces exactly the type of overload necessary to improve the eccentric-to-concentric transition. It forces the muscle to overcome a sudden overload, and then to instantaneously transform that tension into applied power.

Anticipatory Contraction

The second additional neuro-muscular characteristic affected by plyometric training is the capacity of a muscle to anticipate and prepare itself for a sudden stretch. Researchers have noted that, prior to contact, the muscle contracts slightly. This is known as **kinesthetic**, or **anticipatory**, **contraction**. This pre-tensing lets the muscle convert force more efficiently, leading to a more powerful concentric contraction.

To illustrate, consider two balls of the same size, one a tennis ball and the other a superball, and assume they are two identical muscles. The tennis ball represents a muscle that is not pre-tensed before contact; the superball represents a pre-tensed muscle. If we drop the balls from the same height, what happens? The superball—thanks to its pre-tensed state—converts more energy to motion, making it bounce higher.

Pre-tensing allows the muscle to act more like a superball or a tight spring, converting energy into power more effectively.

This tensing of the muscles prior to overload is not usually a conscious act. In fact, if you concentrate on pre-tensing, you inhibit motor performance of the action undertaken. Pre-tensing of the muscles is really an unconscious kinesthetic awareness that helps keep you from being injured and maximizes your ability to perform physically. You probably already know this whether you realize it or not. What's your first reaction when you fall or slip? It's to tense up in anticipation of hitting the ground.

Plyometric training takes advantage of this neuro-muscular awareness to produce greater athletic performance. Through repetition, you develop your kinesthetic ability to pre-tense muscles prior to sudden overload and rapid stretching. This, in effect, helps the muscles "rebound" with greater force, again improving maximum power.

TRAINING MUSCLE ELASTICITY

Increasing muscle activation during an eccentric contraction, achieving faster eccentric-to-concentric transition and improving your ability for anticipatory contraction are the three main neuro-muscular adaptations of plyometric training. Now let's turn our spotlight on a purely physiological adaptation—the conditioning of the elastic properties of the muscle fiber itself.

A concentric contraction is more powerful when preceded by an eccentric contraction, not only due to the stretch reflex but also because of the elastic properties of the muscle. Muscles are like big rubber bands. When a muscle is stretched, the resulting tension stores elastic energy within the muscle. As the muscle contraction switches from eccentric to concentric, this elastic energy is released, adding greater strength to the concentric contraction.

By conditioning the eccentric strength capacity of a muscle, you enable it to store a greater amount of elastic energy for use at the moment the contraction becomes concentric. Studies also show that a fast pre-stretching of the muscle leads to more efficient use of elastic energy, producing even more powerful concentric contractions. Plyometric training develops this elastic strength by suddenly loading, or pre-stretching, the muscle.

❖

The physiology of plyometric training differs dramatically from traditional strength training and weightlifting. Both aim to increase strength and power. But where typical weightlifting relies on *conscious* concentric contraction of the muscle, plyometric training capitalizes on the body's *innate reflexes and instinctive abilities* to maximize explosive power and muscle strength.

❖   ❖   ❖

PLYOMETRIC TRAINING PRINCIPLES

Now that you have a sense how plyometric training accomplishes its magic, let's begin looking at the training principles built into the **Explosive Power** routines. We'll start with the general ones, then move to the more specific.

PROGRESSIVE OVERLOAD

The cornerstone of all conditioning is **progressive overload**. This principle is really a combination of two separate factors, **overload** and **progression**.

Overload

To increase your physical capacity for work and performance, you must force your body to adapt to greater-than-normal stress. **Overloading** is the primary mechanism that causes this adaptation. Overloading simply means forcing muscles to work harder than they are accustomed to. As those muscles adapt to the overload, they become capable of doing even more work.

Too much stress can cause exhaustion or injury. But the right amount of stress increases physical capacity and athletic performance.

The way the body adapts to overload is predictable—which means you can manipulate your training to control your progress. Or, to put that another way, it means that maximum gains in strength and muscle mass result from intelligent planning—not hope, guesswork, or desperation.

Overloading requires working:

- **harder** (lifting heavier weight, running up a steeper slope, and so on)
- **faster** (doing an exercise in less time)
- **longer** (doing more reps, cycling a greater distance or keeping at an exercise longer)

The type of adaptation that occurs depends on the type of overload. Muscles forced to work harder develop greater strength; muscles forced to work faster develop greater speed; muscles forced to work longer develop greater endurance. So when choosing the type of overload to use in training, you must start by identifying the physical capacities and skills you want to develop.

The goal of **Explosive Power** is to maximize strength *and* athletic power.* Since this goal requires developing strength and speed together, the **Explosive Power** training program must force target muscles to work both harder and faster at the same time.

You may be wondering: *Can't I just lift weights more quickly to get this effect?* Not really. "Fast lifting"—even Olympic lifting— doesn't really make muscles work all that much faster, it just makes them work faster than conventional weight training. The great benefit of plyometric training is that the overload occurs in fractions of a second, forcing the muscles to respond both strongly and immediately.

Let's return to our earlier example of someone who trips and falls onto one leg. That one leg suddenly is required to handle the total momentum of the body at a speed faster than walking or running. In a split second, those leg muscles are work-

Types of Overloads

*Later in the *Routines* chapter, we'll see how bodybuilders can use the *Explosive Power* approach to gain muscle mass more quickly, as well.

ing both harder and faster than in nontraining conditions—and even harder and faster than during most other forms of athletic conditioning! This type of two-fold overload, unique to plyometrics, is the key to greater gains.

Progression

Once you adapt to a particular training overload, it's not an overload anymore. The necessary partner of overload, therefore, is **progression**. Progression involves forcing muscles to adapt to higher and higher levels of stress by constantly making them work harder, faster or longer.

To manage progressive overload, you must balance four variables: **mode**, **frequency**, **intensity**, and **duration**. *Mode* is the type of training you do, such as weightlifting, jumping, or running. *Frequency* is the number of times you train within a given time frame. For example, you might weight train with a frequency of three times per week. *Intensity* measures the degree of exertion, or how hard you force yourself to work. In weight training, intensity is measured as a percentage of maximum strength performed within a given time frame. *Duration* is the length of time or number of repetitions for a particular exercise. Maintaining a progressive overload requires increasing the values of one or more of these variables. We will be manipulating three of the four (frequency, intensity and duration) in the *Routines* chapter.

VARIATION

When you begin any type of strength or power training, your central nervous system is "shocked" into response as part of the adaptation process. This makes for substantial initial increases in strength and performance. (Remember the amazing gains you experienced when you first started weight training?) Over time, though, your body gets used to the overload and progress plateaus. To bring continuing improvements, any program needs to be changed somewhat every few weeks.* Variability is equally important in plyometric training. As effective as plyometric exercises are at shocking the central nervous system into an adaptive response, they must be changed periodically to remain effective.

*There are some exceptions to this rule having to do with advanced bodybuilding routines.

Contrary to popular belief, you make your gains from training during the recovery periods *between* workouts. So rest is a vital component of the formula for athletic success. Indeed, heavy training with little rest all but guarantees fatigue, injuries and frustration.

That goes double for plyometric training. The demands it places on the central nervous system and the eccentric capacity of muscle fibers make it much more stressful than conventional weight training. You need a *minimum* of 48 hours to recover from a hard plyometric workout. Once again, remember—you grow while you rest, not while you train.

RECOVERY & RESTORATION

Just as no doctor would prescribe the same medicine for everyone, no one plyometric program will work for every athlete. Size, age, and physical condition substantially affect the type and amount of training you should do. In the *Schedule* chapter, we'll discuss guidelines for picking your optimum routine.

INDIVIDUALITY

To meet the strenuous demands of plyometric exercise, you need to start out with adequate basic muscular strength. The exercises use momentum and gravity to create a sudden, intense muscular overload—**If you don't begin with adequate basic strength, you could be injured.**

How much beginning strength do you need? For the most demanding forms of plyometric training (such as certain *power* plyometric exercises), we endorse the accepted recommendation that you be able to squat 150% to 200% of your bodyweight. For the less strenuous parts of this program, though, 4 to 6 months on a comprehensive weightlifting program such as that in **Secrets of Advanced Bodybuilders** should suffice.

BASIC STRENGTH

RATE OF STRETCH VS. DEGREE OF STRETCH

For an exercise to trigger the stretch reflex, it must overload the target muscle *rapidly*. Remember, the *rate* of speed with which you stretch the target muscle is much more important than *how far* you stretch the muscle during overload.

For example: When doing plyometric Push-Ups, you should explode upward quickly and forcefully immediately after contact. Unlike the form you use during common Push-Ups, you don't want to sink all the way down and touch your chest to the ground. Likewise, you should make all jumping movements quick and bouncy, like a kangaroo. Slow jumps where you sink deep into a squat negate the plyometric effect. (Such exercises are certainly dynamic, but they are not plyometric.)

Successful plyometric training depends on the quickness of execution. It's the speed of the stretch that counts!

EXPLOSIVE EXECUTION

In plyometric training, you want to train as many muscle fibers as possible. This requires a conscious effort on your part. Concentrate on reacting explosively following the eccentric movement. Don't gather or wind up before before the concentric explosion.

Like any ballistic exercise, plyometric movements carry some risk of muscle strain and injury. Creating strong eccentric contractions through rapid overloading of the muscle puts tremendous strain on the muscles, joints, ligaments and tendons.

Proper execution and a gradual increase in intensity over time are essential to reduce your risk of injury and overtraining! Remember—plyometric exercises often deceive you into believing that your muscles are not tired. Because plyos are physiologically different from weightlifting, they don't create the intense burn and pump that accompany that form of training. Typically, your muscles seem dead and heavy the day *after* you do a plyometric workout, but feel just fine during the training session.

The following general guidelines will help you build greater speed and strength while avoiding the pitfalls of overtraining and injury:

■ Approach plyometric training conservatively. Regardless of your basic strength, begin plyometric training by doing the most general exercises at low intensity. Your body must become familiar with a totally new type of very demanding training. Follow the gradual progression through the levels of the program. Don't skip levels! You will make greater gains if you build a solid foundation for more advanced work.

■ Proper technique and intensity underlie good plyometric training. Sloppy, high-volume workouts will not lead to better results. Let good technique be your guide—when form deteriorates, stop for the day!

■ Plyometric exercises should always be done on soft, level surfaces. Grass fields and gymnastic mats work best. Avoid hard surfaces like concrete, asphalt, tennis courts, and wooden floors.

■ Use shoes with good support and a cushioned heel and mid-sole.

■ Don't increase resistance by using weight vests or wrist and ankle weights. Added resistance forces you to spend more time absorbing the overload, slowing the transition from eccentric to concentric muscle contractions. Since the speed of this transition is what you are training, adding weight defeats your purpose. *Plyometric exercise is not weightlifting; it is a different type of training altogether.*

That does it for the theory. Time to put what you now know about plyometric training into practice!

❖　　　❖　　　❖

PART TWO

Training

THE EXERCISES

Most athletic movement can be described in terms of four characteristics: rhythm (or coordination), speed, power, and endurance. In successful plyometric training, exercises must be tailored for these specific qualities. This chapter describes all the exercises in the **Explosive Power** programs, and discusses how they can be applied to your specific goals.

TYPES OF PLYOMETRICS

Rhythm Plyometrics

No matter what your sport, you need **rhythm.** Why? Because rhythm, also described as *coordination*, frames all athletic performance. It is the basis upon which speed and strength are built.

Rhythm drills help develop the type of basic strength needed to perform complex movements *explosively.* Often, even athletes with big muscles have little ability to transform strength into coordinated movement. Rhythm plyos teach you to use your strength effectively.

For the most part, rhythm plyometrics are simple drills that emphasize easy, flowing movement. These drills often incorporate a single element of a more difficult and complex movement.

Speed Plyometrics

Some of the most interesting new ideas in sports concern speed training. Although old-school thinking held that you must live with the speed you were born with, recent research suggests that the potential exists to increase one's basic speed capacity. While genetics does have a big effect on how fast you are, qualities like muscle contractile strength and synchronization capacity can be developed through training to make you faster and more explosive.

In speed plyometrics, the overload principle is fulfilled by shortening the time frame in which the exercise takes place. As a consequence, your neuro-muscular system learns to respond more rapidly to stimuli. The result: greater physical speed and quickness.

Like rhythm drills, many speed exercises isolate single movements at speeds faster than normal. Hopping and bounding drills stress extremely quick reaction from the ground. Speed-assisted exercises done with a towing device force you to perform more complex movements at speeds greater than you can reach alone.

Think of the implications of increasing speed. Speed is the single most important factor in athletic success. In any given sport, all things being equal, speed wins. Moreover, speed is a vital component of explosive power. For jumping, hitting, or running, speed and strength combine to determine performance.

Power Plyometrics

If you are familiar with plyometric exercise at all, you probably are acquainted with power plyometrics. Traditionally, power drills have made up the core of plyometric training. These exercises build explosive strength for sports requiring effort against resistance. Weightlifters, boxers, and tennis players, for example, all need the explosive strength that power plyos offer.

Power drills call for great intensity of effort and execution. Usually, you perform relatively few repetitions at one time, concentrating on explosive movement. The goal is not to maximize the number of repetitions, but to exact the most out of each single effort.

Power plyos for the lower body include a number of jumping movements such as hops, bounds, single and multiple jumps, and box depth jumps. For the upper body, they include various medicine ball throws, heavy bag work, and body weight exercises like Power Push-Ups.

Power-Endurance Plyometrics

Plyometric training does not specifically build endurance—that is, the type of stamina used by long-distance runners, cyclists, and cross-country skiers. However, plyos can help you attain endurance of a different sort. Many sports require you to be explosive time and time again. The boxer or martial artist must deliver powerful blows and kicks over the course of many rounds. Basketball and volleyball players need leaping ability throughout long games and matches. Done right, plyometric training can help build that specific type of **power-endurance.**

Building power-endurance through plyos involves many of the same exercises done to develop rhythm and speed. To stress the endurance aspect, the exercises are performed at medium to low intensity with numerous repetitions and additional sets.

THE RHYTHM PLYOMETRIC EXERCISES

Rhythm Skips

Description

Skipping is one plyometric exercise that nearly everyone has done at some time. Rhythm Skips help develop awareness of body position and movement. The coordination required helps create good mechanics for running and jumping along with a sense of fluid rhythm. Rhythm Skips serve as a basic exercise for all levels of the **Explosive Power** program.

Like most plyometric drills, Rhythm Skips are a total-body exercise. A wide range of muscle groups are affected, as well as the entire neuro-muscular system. However, most of the work is done by lower-body muscles, primarily the gluteus, quadriceps, hamstrings, calf muscles, and hip flexors.

Rhythm Skips help build basic strength and are an excellent warm-up drill for all plyo sessions.

Execution

Following one or two walk-in steps, initiate a skip-step with either leg. A skip-step is a small, short hop on one foot. With the opposite leg, drive the knee upward to waist level. Upon landing on the skip, step forward with the opposite leg and repeat the initial motion. The arms should swing long and loose, with the hands coming to shoulder level at each swing forward and back. The upper body should be tall and erect. Don't lean backward.

Think hips up, eyes up!

Emphasize driving the free leg waist high with the lower leg relaxed and kept behind the knee. Don't reach forward with the foot. The support leg should extend fully as you drive up onto the balls of the feet. Most importantly, the motion off the ground should be quick. It isn't important that you skip high off the ground, but that you emphasize a smooth, quick rhythm as you skip.

Fig. 9 — Rhythm Skips

High-Knee Runs

Description

Most sports involve running, and high-knee drills are especially useful for learning proper running mechanics. Good running form lets you use speed and power most efficiently. Moreover, High-Knee Runs develop overall coordination and quickness.

High-Knee Running is an overall body exercise, incorporating the muscles of the shoulders, arms, and legs. Most specifically, High-Knee Runs target the hip flexor muscles. This drill is especially appropriate for speed-oriented athletes—especially martial artists, for whom strong, fast hip flexors help create the lightning-quick strength needed to deliver effective kicks.

Execution

High-Knee Running is similar to running in place, although you move forward at a slow walking pace. Begin by running in place, and then let yourself start to move forward slowly. Focus on driving your knees up to waist level or a bit higher. Swing your arms quickly in sync with your leg turnover. Drive your arms as if you were sprinting: elbows bent at approximately 90 degrees, hands coming up to eye level, elbows moving behind the body on the backswing.

The running motion should be fluid, but not necessarily fast. Your body position should be tall, with the head looking forward. You should not feel as if you are jumping or lunging from step to step. Don't reach out with the lower leg as you move forward. Focus only on the piston-like movement of

Fig. 10 — High-Knee Runs

your arms and legs. Running in place will remedy any tendency to reach forward with the lower legs.

One very common mistake with High-Knee Running is leaning backward while trying to bring the knees to waist level. Doing so will only ruin the rhythmic intent of the exercise. Always make sure that your hips and chest stay tall and forward to get the most out of High-Knee Runs.

Butt Kicks

Description

Butt Kicks are the counterpart of High-Knee Running. Like High-Knee Runs, they develop coordinated running movement and mechanics while building strength and flexibility.

Butt Kicks condition the hamstring muscles in the back of the leg. All too often, there is a serious strength imbalance between the quadriceps and the hamstrings. Such an imbalance can lead to injury and tears of the hamstring muscles, as well as problems for the lower back. Greater dynamic hamstring strength contributes to more explosive athletic performance and, at the same time, it protects the body from the demands of such hard effort.

Special Note for Martial Artists: Dynamic hamstring strength is especially vital for developing the explosive kicks and sweeps of the martial artist. The fast, snappy kicks in Savate, Tae Kwon Do, and numerous other styles place tremendous strain on the lower hamstring muscles around the knee. Strengthening these muscles is essential.

Execution

There are two ways to do this exercise.

In the first method, assume good running posture: tall, with your weight on the balls of your feet. Focus on kicking the butt or glutes with each foot as you run forward. As with High-Knee Runs, move forward at a slow walking pace. Your knees should point down toward the ground. Drive your arms as if sprinting. As with High-Knee Running, the execution of Butt Kicks should be fluid and quick, emphasizing smoothness over speed.

The second method combines Butt Kicks with High-Knee Running. The aim here is to kick the butt with the foot while driving the knee up to waist level. Keep the same arm action and pace of movement. This method requires greater coordination, flexibility, and rhythm, so become proficient with the first method before trying this one.

Fig. 11 — Butt Kick #1

Fig. 12 — Butt Kick #2

Ankle Bounces

Description

To use leg power efficiently, you need a powerful base of support in the muscles, tendons, and ligaments of the calves and ankles. In sports involving jumping and running, every contact with the ground transfers force directly through the lower legs. Likewise, most martial arts, including boxing, require strength and endurance for staying balanced on the balls of the feet.

Ankle Bounces strengthen the *soleus* and *gastrocnemius* muscles of the calf along with the Achilles' tendons and other small ankle muscles.

Execution

Stand with your hands on your hips. Rise onto the balls of your feet and bounce, flexing only at the ankles. Keep the knees as straight as possible throughout. Once you become accustomed to bouncing without bending the knees, include some forward and lateral movement with each bounce jump. Be quick off the ground; don't settle with each bounce.

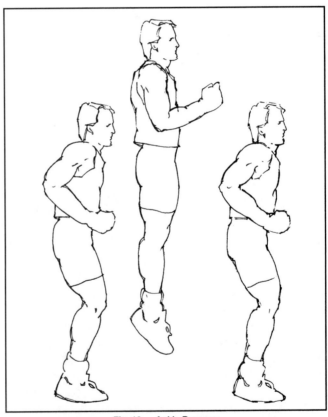

Fig. 13 — Ankle Bounces

Jumping Rope

Description

Like Ankle Bounces, jumping rope builds coordination of the feet and arms. It is an excellent and time-honored method of creating good rhythmic foot movement for almost all sports. (For a complete jump rope program, see the *Jumping Rope* chapter in *Health For Life*'s **MAX O$_2$** training manual.)

Execution

Jumping rope can be done in a number of ways. If you are new to jumping rope, first get comfortable with the basic coordination required to do the exercise. Combining simple ankle bounces with a twirling rope is the first step. After that, alternate skipping in place over the rope. You can improve the exercise by varying the speed of the rope in intervals or by adding extra movements to gain better coordination and rhythm.

Fig. 14 — Jumping Rope

Fig. 15 — Skipping Rope

Skipping Kicks

Description

Skipping Kicks are an advanced rhythm plyometric exercise. They are excellent for developing coordination and body awareness because they require many integrated movements. Martial artists who need to combine punching, striking, and kicking benefit greatly from this type of rhythm work. Skiers, football players, and others engaged in complex movement sports should do this exercise as well.

The exercise coordinates the muscle action of the hip flexors, quadriceps, hamstrings, and ankles with arm swing. With practice, the muscles learn the synchronized flow of multiple quick movements.

Execution

Begin skipping in the manner described for Rhythm Skips. Now, as the knee is driven to waist level, extend the lower leg—"kick" the foot straight out from the body—so that the leg is roughly parallel to the ground. From there, pull the foot and leg back actively so that the foot returns to the ground beneath the rest of the body. As the foot lands, the next skip begins. The arms are held with the elbow angles at about 90 degrees, and should move in sync with the legs. Opposite arms and legs should move in the same direction.

The forward pace of these skips will be slower than for other skips, but the overall speed of movement will be faster. As with High-Knee Running, make sure you don't lean back as you drive the knee and kick the foot. If anything, you should lean forward slightly to counteract the force of the kick.

Fig. 16 — Skipping Kicks

Rhythm Bounds

Description

This exercise introduces you to the bounding and jumping of power and speed plyometric training in the form of a rhythm drill. Rhythm Bounds are an excellent way to build basic dynamic strength. The relatively low intensity of this type of bounding allows you to do more repetitions without overtraining or risking injury. Rhythm Bounds are also a good way to train for power-endurance.

Bounding strengthens all the muscles of the lower body, especially the quadriceps and glutes. Because bounding develops general strength, you can benefit from this exercise no matter which sport you play. As a highly effective functional strength exercise, bounding actually stimulates overall strength gains! Doing bounds in rhythm mode builds coordination and power simultaneously.

Bounds are leaps from one foot to another, stressing a quick impulse off the ground. A bound is more or less a jumping running stride; however, you spend more time off the ground between foot contacts than you do with normal running or sprinting. You should push forcefully off the ground and drive the knee up and forward vigorously. Done properly, bounding feels as if you are floating between footfalls.

If you are new to plyometric exercise, bounding may be unfamiliar to you. Many people have a hard time learning to bound because they tend to reach with their legs as if they are running. Here is an easy way to learn:

Start by bouncing on the balls of your feet. Then, bounce from one foot to the next. At the same time, get used to swinging your arms (as if running) in cadence with each bounce from foot to foot. When this becomes comfortable, start moving each foot a bit in front of the other with each bounce. Slowly increase the distance covered by each bounce. Try to get to the point where you can bounce easily from foot to foot while driving the knee of the free leg to waist level. Notice that sensation of hanging in the air the other with each bounce. Slowly increase the distance covered by each bounce. Try to get to the point where you can bounce easily from foot to foot while driving the knee of the free leg to waist level. Notice that sensation of hanging in the air for a brief moment? Good. You're bounding!

Execution

Start the exercise with a few jogging strides. Leap from the ground off one leg while driving the opposite knee up toward the chest. The support leg should extend fully with a quick impulse off the ground while the knee on the free leg drives up to waist level or more. Hold this position momentarily until the body starts to return to the ground. Don't let the lower leg drift out in front of the knee as it approaches the ground. As the body descends, initiate the next bound with another quick push from the ground. The arms should move with the legs as if you were running.

Don't strain to maximize the height or length of each bound. Instead, try to move quickly and smoothly along the ground. Concentrate on smooth execution and technique. The power comes next.

Fig. 17 — Rhythm Bounds

THE SPEED PLYOMETRIC EXERCISES

Some of the most interesting recent advances in strength and power training have come in the area of speed development. Research suggests that speed is much more trainable than was previously thought. The basis of speed plyometric training is the use of *overspeed* (shortening the period of time in which a movement is performed), to fulfill the overload principle. In other words, you make the body adapt to speeds with which it is not accustomed. By doing so, you increase your overall capacity for speed and power.

All types of plyometric exercise condition the body's neuromuscular system. However, while power plyos focus primarily on explosive strength, speed plyos concentrate upon the time component of power. As such, speed plyos train the body's central nervous system, allowing you to recruit and apply muscle strength more efficiently.

Speed is the lifeblood of most sports. Every running step, strike, or jump occurs in just a fraction of a second. A good athlete needs the ability to summon strength instantaneously. Speed plyometrics teach you to do just that.

Speed-Rhythm exercises condition the neuro-muscular system for speed and coordination. Rhythm and coordination are necessary to use speed-strength most efficiently. Exercises incorporating both elements simultaneously develop this capacity.

The rhythm plyometric exercises discussed earlier are converted into speed training by emphasizing extremely quick movement through a shorter range of motion.

Execution

Use the same positions and mechanics as described for the rhythm forms of these drills. With High-Knee Runs, attempt to drive the knees up, but focus on rapid turnover. The arms and legs should have one-half to two-thirds the normal range of motion. Butt Kicks should also stress rapid repetition, again, with a shortened range of motion. Skips should be done purely for speed, not distance. The rhythm of the exercise should be extremely quick—the skips will seem like a fast shuffle.

Description

Speed Hops provide overspeed training for the entire lower body and arms stressing minimum contact time with the ground. They are an extremely effective exercise for all athletes.

Execution

Speed Hops are done in basically the same manner as a two-leg Power Hop. Jump up, driving the arms and knees vigorously, and pull the feet towards the buttocks. Make sure that the arms swing quickly alongside the body. Don't let them circle like a bird taking flight.

There should be no forward movement. Concentrate on getting off the ground as fast as possible. Use your arms to initiate your hop. Don't pause at all as your feet touch the ground at the end of each repetition. Minimizing your time on the ground is most important.

Remember that with Power Hops you were asked to visualize a kangaroo in motion. Well, with Speed Hops you want to envision the speedy hopping of a rabbit. *Be as fast as possible.*

Speed-Rhythm Exercises: High-Knee Runs, Butt Kicks, Skips

Speed Hops

Fig. 18 — Speed Hops

SPEED-ASSISTED TRAINING

The sport of track and field has used speed-assisted or overspeed training with good results for some time. In this type of training, you are forced to move at speeds faster than you can generate on your own. Your neuro-muscular system adapts to this hypernormal speed. As a result you become faster.

Typically, overspeed training makes use of an apparatus that pulls you along a little faster than you can run alone. A number of such products are sold for this purpose.

An overspeed training device usually consists of a harness or belt with a thick elastic cord or rubber tubing attached. Wearing the harness, and fixing the loose end of tubing on a stationary object (or attaching it to a partner), you stretch the elastic, and then sprint, bound, or hop in the direction of the pull. The stretched tubing pulls you along faster than if you were unassisted, forcing you to complete the distance in less time.

Assisted Sprints

Execution

Do sprints on a running track or a level playing field free of dangerous ruts or holes. Stretch the tubing so that you feel tension pulling against you. When you start sprinting, concentrate on quick, efficient running form. If you feel yourself braking against the pull of the tubing, reduce the amount of tension at the start.

It's best to do assisted sprints with a partner. Have your partner stretch the cord. Then, upon command, both of you start running, your partner in the lead. This ensures a more consistent and controllable pull from the tubing. Sprints of 50 to 80 meters are recommended.

If you train alone, attach the other end to a secure object like a tree or post—and be sure, when sprinting, not to run into it!

Fig. 19 — Assisted Sprints (with partner)

Description

You can do assisted bounding and hopping to develop speed and power together.

Assisted Bounds & Hops

Execution

Using an elastic device, do a normal set of Power Bounds or Hops. The elastic will pull you along, forcing you to be fast with these power movements. Once again, limit the tension of the cord so that it does not keep you from doing the exercise properly.

Downhill Running

Description

Downhill running can also be used for overspeed training. In this case, the force of gravity pulls you along to make you move faster.

Execution

You can boost running speed by sprinting on a slight downhill grade of 2 or 3 degrees. Make sure not to choose a surface with too severe a grade—this will only force you to brake your speed to keep from running out of control.

Speed Plyometrics for Martial Artists

Doing specific speed-assisted training for the martial arts is difficult and potentially dangerous. Isolating the arms and legs for overspeed punching and kicking is impractical. Moreover, it's easy to hyperextend your knees, elbows, wrists or shoulders because you have so little control against the tension of any elastic device. For these reasons, we don't recommend that you try assisted strikes and kicks.

The good news is that much of martial arts training already stresses speed punching and kicking. These drills do, in fact, involve a certain amount of plyometric activity. Punching and kicking done rapidly with a short range of motion develop speed for the martial artist. Also, rapid multiple repetitions of a particular kick or punch have a plyometric effect for those muscles.

Lastly, the speed plyometric drills described above are excellent general speed exercises. Though not specific to punching and kicking, they do increase your overall speed-strength and quickness.

Power plyometrics are among the most intense and explosive exercises you can do. Be careful! Always make sure that you are properly warmed-up and have stretched and loosened the muscles in preparation. When starting power-oriented drills, be conservative; proceed gradually.

Two rules of thumb will help you determine if you are ready to do power plyos.

- **Rule One:** You should be able to perform the exercise as a rhythm drill at low intensity first.
- **Rule Two:** You should be able to do the exercise with good technique. Poor technique means you aren't ready for that exercise.

Description

Unlike Rhythm Skips, which stress fluid horizontal movement, Power Skips stress a vertical impulse off the ground and are performed with much greater intensity and effort. Power Skips should be done with deliberate concentration on powerful movement.

THE POWER PLYOMETRIC EXERCISES

Lower Body

Power Skips

Fig. 20 — Power Skips

Execution

Begin as you would for Rhythm Skips. In Power Skips, however, the drive from the support leg and the knee drive of the free leg should be vigorous and explosive. The arms drive powerfully, and are held as if you were sprinting. Aim for maximum height and distance with each skip. Try to maintain smooth technique, but focus on power. Remember to rebound as fast as possible off the ground!

Two-Leg Power Hops

Description

The Two-Leg Hop is an excellent general power exercise that serves as a good introduction to explosive training. Most beginners can do this drill rather easily. Like most plyos, hops are a functional strength exercise affecting a wide range of muscle groups.

Execution

Stand relaxed and upright with your head up and eyes looking forward. Lean slightly forward with your upper body, and bend your arms, holding your hands with thumbs pointed up. Begin by jumping up as high as possible. Drive your arms vigorously as you jump. As you leave the ground, your knees should be pulled up as high as possible with your feet pulled towards the buttocks.

As you land, repeat the jump stressing height and quickness off the ground. You should not pause or "gather" between jumps.

Modified technique: If you're just starting out, true Power Hops may be too difficult to do correctly. To avoid frustration and/or injury, experiment with the following modifications to make this exercise easier.

First, you can insert a very small hop between each Power Hop. This enables you to adjust your body and prepare for the next full hop. Using a small intermediary hop will make your introduction to power plyos much easier.

Second, as you progress to consecutive hops, you may want to reduce their intensity—or the intensity of every *other* hop—until you feel comfortable doing every hop with full effort.

Fig. 21 — Two-Leg Power Hops

Imagine a kangaroo hopping across the Australian outback. These animals are the perfect example of plyometric hopping. Your goal when doing Power Hops should be to demonstrate the same kind of continuous explosive strength!

Description

Power Bounding is perhaps the most familiar of plyometric exercises. Track and field athletes use bounding extensively in their training because it so effectively builds explosive power in the lower body. And, since it so closely mimics the mechanics of running, power bounding is beneficial for all sports.

Execution

The Power Bound is simply a more intense and explosive version of the Rhythm Bound described earlier. With each bound, you should attempt to cover as much distance as possible using good technique. Get the feel of hanging in the air, and then exploding back off the ground immediately upon contact. When doing Power Bounds, land more or less flat-footed on each contact. This prevents injury to the feet and ankles.

Arm action should be the same as with Rhythm Bounds, although a double-arm drive is acceptable. With a double-arm

Power Bounds

drive, avoid flapping your arms like a bird in order to keep your balance, as this reduces the amount of power off the ground you can generate.

Fig. 22 — Power Bounds

One-Leg Hops

Description

One-Leg Hops are an advanced power plyometric exercise that requires substantial strength, balance and coordination. They are physically very demanding, and you should do them only after progressing through the other levels of the *Explosive Power* program. You should be quite proficient at Two-Leg Hops before starting one-leg exercises.

Execution

One-Leg Hops are done much like Two-Leg Hops, except that it is even more important to cycle the knees and feet through quickly. Since you won't get the same height as with Two-Leg Hops, the movement is even faster. Nonetheless, try to drive each knee up and bring your foot to your buttocks with each hop. The exercise should be continuous, with a quick push-off from the ground.

As with Two-Leg Hops, beginners should insert a very small one-leg hop between each full hop.

Don't underestimate the physical stress of One-Leg Hops! You can injure yourself easily if you don't approach this exercise carefully. Stop the exercise if it produces any pain in the hip, knee, or ankle.

Fig. 23 — One-Leg Hops

Description

Many sports, such as basketball, skiing, tennis, and volleyball, require you to move laterally, or side-to-side. Conventional weight training doesn't really address the strength needed for lateral movement sports. Side Hops are quite specific to these sports. They will help you develop the ballistic strength in the lower body needed to move explosively and quickly from side to side.

Execution

Start in a relaxed standing position. Load the jump as if you were going to start a Two-Leg Hop. However, instead of jumping up and forward, jump up and sideways. Drive the arms up, pulling the knees up and bringing the feet up under the buttocks. Repeat the jump immediately upon reaching the

Two-Leg Side Hops

ground. Try to get maximum height and explosion with each jump. Don't pause between jumps.

Side Hops are easier to do if you use some sort of obstacle to jump over. An obstacle provides visual reference and stimulus for the exercise. Plastic traffic cones work well; they come in various sizes and provide little risk if you hit them while jumping. You can also set several cones in a row, so you can move forward as you jump from side-to-side. Never use an obstacle that is fixed or one that could injure you if you hit it.

Fig. 24 — Two-Leg Side Hops

Technique hint: Moving side-to-side will be easier if you lean slightly inward with your shoulders as you jump. Of course, you need to continually adjust your body position from one side to the other. Also, driving your arms across your body somewhat will make the lateral movement easier and more efficient. Remember to be quick as well as powerful with each jump.

Description

Alternate-Leg Side Hops are side-to-side hops done from one leg to another. This exercise requires greater single leg strength, balance, and coordination than Two-Leg Side Hops. It closely mimics the types of moves used in a wide range of sports.

Execution

From a relaxed starting position, hop laterally, pushing off with your outside leg and driving your inside leg up so that the knee comes to waist level or higher. Reverse this action once the inside foot has returned to the ground. Make sure to drive the inside knee up as you hop. Don't just reach out to the side with the foot. Keep the motion quick and powerful, moving continuously throughout the exercise.

Alternate-Leg Side Hops

Fig. 25 — Alternate-Leg Side Hops

Box Jumps

Description

Box Jumps are also called Depth Jumps. They are among the most demanding plyometric exercises and can pose a significant risk of injury if not done intelligently and cautiously. These exercises are recommended only for highly trained athletes with excellent basic strength.

Execution

From an elevated box or platform, drop down onto a soft surface such as grass or a gymnastics mat. Landing in a slightly squatted position, immediately rebound with a two-leg jump as high and quick as possible. One or two additional jumps can be added to the initial jump.

Fig. 26 — Box Jumps

The height of the box or platform should be determined according to your ability. To avoid any serious risk of injury, we recommend never using a platform higher than 18 inches. Start from a relatively small height of about 12 inches. Progress slowly, a few inches at a time. Be assured that doing these jumps properly from low heights will still give you very good results. Don't risk your training investment by trying to jump from too great a height!

Upper Body

Medicine Ball Tosses

Description

Medicine balls have been around for a very long time. Many of us can remember those old heavy, crusty leather balls stuffed somewhere in the old high school or college gymnasium. Before weight training became popular, a lot of strength training was done with medicine balls.

Well, they're back! It turns out that medicine balls are tremendously effective at building dynamic upper-body strength and explosive power. And whether you are a bodybuilder, tennis player, basketball player, volleyball player or martial artist, explosive upper-body strength is crucial for maximum performance!

Medicine balls come in a range of weights and sizes, and you should choose the ones that seem right for your frame and strength. If anything, choose balls that seem a bit on the light side. Balls that are too heavy will slow the exercise and negate the plyometric effect. Usually, two or three different weighted balls are all you need.

(Medicine balls in 2-, 3-, 4-, and 5-kg weights are available from a number of sports supply companies, including *Health For Life*.)

Medicine ball tosses can be done standing, kneeling, sitting, or even lying on your back. It helps to have a partner who can feed the ball to you in order to enhance the plyometric effect.

Standing Overhead Tosses

Description

The Standing Overhead Toss is an excellent exercise that trains the upper- *and* lower-body muscles involved in throwing. Almost all the muscles of the trunk, shoulders, and arms work together in this exercise.

Execution

Stand erect with feet even and slightly spread. (As you progress, alternate standing with one foot forward to vary the exercise.) Holding the ball overhead with both hands, bring it behind the head as far as possible in one smooth motion. As you reach back, let the elbows bend a little. Once you feel a stretch of the upper-body muscles, pull forward and throw the ball.

The key to this exercise is quick initiation of the toss. Don't let the medicine ball come to rest as you extend behind your head. On the other hand, don't use a fast jerky wind-up, or you may hurt yourself. Use smooth rhythm reaching back, and then give an explosive toss forward!

If you have the assistance of a training partner, have him or her drop or lightly toss the ball into your hands. Your arms should already be extended behind your head, waiting for the ball. The instant you feel the ball hit your hands, initiate the toss.

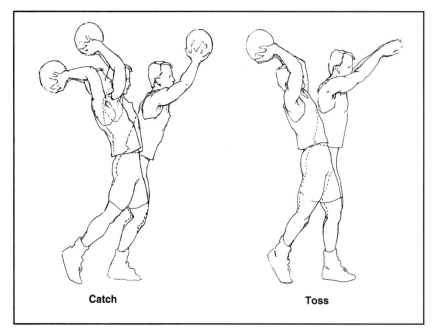

Catch   **Toss**

Fig. 27 — Medicine Ball Standing Overhead Tosses

Description

This exercise is identical to the Standing Toss except that you do it while kneeling. This further isolates the muscles of the upper body and prevents you from using your legs to generate power.

In the Kneeling Toss, *be careful not to bend backwards too far.* This can easily happen if you overreach with the ball extended behind your head, and may cause back injury. Remember that the *rate* of stretch is more important than the degree of stretch.

Kneeling Overhead Tosses

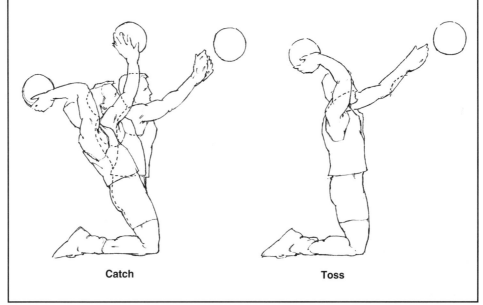

Catch   Toss

Fig. 28 — Medicine Ball Kneeling Overhead Toss

Description

The Push Pass isolates the chest and shoulder muscles in much the same way as the Bench Press. It is a very useful exercise for those involved in any type of contact sport, including martial artists seeking greater punching power.

Execution

Stand tall with the feet slightly apart. Hold the ball somewhat out in front of your chest. Draw the ball in toward the chest, then push it away in one quick and powerful thrust.

Push Passes

Again, it helps to have a partner feed the ball to you. In any case, the "catch" should be fast. Don't let the ball come to rest against your chest. Make sure that you use a ball light enough to pass quickly. Don't worry about attaining maximum distance. Proper and explosive execution are the key to the best gains.

The best way to do Push Passes is lying on the ground. That way you can perform the repetitions of the exercise continuously. If you have a partner, have him or her drop the medicine ball to you from a height that allows you to do the exercise properly.

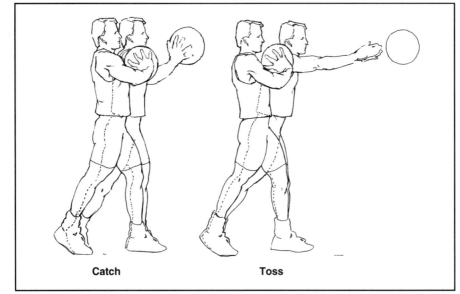

Catch   Toss

Fig. 29 — Medicine Ball Push Passes

Twist Tosses

Description

Medicine Ball Twist Tosses are superb for developing rotational power in the trunk and shoulders. Sports like baseball, tennis, and of course the martial arts demand explosive rotation of the upper body.

Execution

Assume an open stance. Hold the medicine ball in both hands with the arms extended and relaxed. Rotate your upper body, holding the ball in front of your body. Turn until you feel a good stretch, then immediately rotate the upper body forward, throwing the ball. The throw should start from the hips and trunk, with the arms trailing—in effect, you *sling* the ball rather than throw it.

Fig. 30 — Medicine Ball Twist Tosses

Power Push-Ups

Description

For many of us, the Push-Up was our first strength training exercise. Power Push-Ups are a variation of the classic Push-Up. They emphasizes a fast, explosive thrust in which the hands actually leave the ground.

This may sound a lot like Push-Ups with a clap; however, the range of motion in Power Push-Ups is smaller and the entire action faster. In fact, each push upward is similar to a hit or quick shove off the ground.

Power Push-Ups build tremendous explosive power in the chest, shoulders and arms. The exercise forces you to reverse your downward momentum in very little time. Obviously, martial artists, boxers, football players, and throwers who need explosive upper-body strength will benefit greatly from this exercise.

Moreover, bodybuilders and weightlifters can reap significant gains from this exercise. Later, we'll discuss exactly how you can combine plyometric training with your weight training routine to reach new levels of strength and muscle mass.

Execution

Power Push-Ups should be done forcefully and quickly. The tendency is to spend too much time in contact with the ground. Don't worry about achieving a full range of motion. Concern yourself, instead, with producing a truly explosive reaction upon ground contact. Spending too much time moving through a long range of motion negates the plyometric nature of the exercise.

Assume a standard Push-Up position, face down, toes touching the ground, and your hands placed slightly wider than your shoulders. Push up forcefully, causing your hands to lose contact with the ground. Don't extend your arms fully, but keep them slightly bent in anticipation of returning to the ground. As your hands contact the ground, repeat the push as explosively as possible. The exercise should feel as if you are bouncing off your hands.

Fig. 31 —Power Push-Ups

Power Push-Ups are hard work! Don't fret; few athletes can do full Power Push-Ups properly. If at first you are not able to do them from a full Push-Up position, start by using your knees as a base. You will still be able to put great stress on the muscles of the chest and upper body.

Slow execution of Power Push-Ups ruins the exercise. Don't force yourself to do the exercise from full position if it slows you down. Likewise, don't sacrifice explosiveness for extra range of motion or depth. As you gain strength, you will be able to handle a deeper, more pre-stretched position upon contact.

Power Push-Ups will not produce the "pump" or "burn" that typical Push-Ups do. They shouldn't! Nonetheless, they put tremendous stress on the muscles, tendons, and ligaments of the arms, shoulders, and chest. As with any power exercise: Be cautious!

Fig. 32 —Kneeling Power Push-Ups

POWER PLYOMETRIC EXERCISES FOR THE MARTIAL ARTIST (USING THE HEAVY BAG)

Plyometric training is perfect for the martial artist. In a genre that demands maximum power with blinding speed, the speed-strength provided by plyos are exactly what the martial artist needs. Earlier in the book, we discussed the various forms of functional strength. The starting and explosive strength developed by plyometric exercise helps you use your greatest strength in the shortest time possible.

Martial artists and boxers usually get some plyometric training every time they do a heavy bag workout. Every punch and kick into the bag loads the muscle very rapidly. Although your muscles are already contracting concentrically, the sudden contact creates an overload and intensifies the activity, producing greater power and strength.

Using your heavy bag in some new ways will let you train plyometrically to gain greater power and speed in all your strikes and punches.

The keys to using the heavy bag for plyometric training are: one, using the momentum from a swinging bag, and two, initiating your punch or kick as a response to overload from contact with the bag.

With heavy bag plyos, you take advantage of momentum from a moving bag rather than relying on gravity and your body weight. Using the heavy bag allows you to mimic specific positions and motions used in the strikes and kicks of any martial art. So, not only do you develop greater general power, you gain specific explosiveness for your discipline.

As a general rule, heavy bag plyos don't involve full strikes, punches, or kicks. Instead, they focus on the quick transition from eccentric load to concentric contraction. Don't worry about driving through the bag with a long, powerful thrust; focus only on the instant of contact.

Heavy Bag Pushes

Description

Heavy Bag Pushes build punching power and core trunk strength. The muscles of the chest, shoulders, and triceps do most of the work.

Execution

Heavy Bag Pushes are similar to Medicine Ball Push Passes. Here you should emphasize a fast "catch" and push of the bag. Stand in on-guard position. Push the heavy bag away from you to set it swinging a bit. As it returns, catch the bag with both hands, pushing it away as fast and explosively as possible. This contact should occur at the point where the bag crosses through the vertical axis, so you will be absorbing much of its momentum. The push-off should seem somewhat

Fig. 33 — Heavy Bag Pushes

like a punch—or as though you are bouncing the bag off your hands. Repeat for the desired number of repetitions.

Description

Heavy Bag Hits are similar to the pushes described above, but are done single-handed and stress greater punching action. The goal of this exercise is to train explosive punching power.

Execution:

Stand in on-guard position. Push the bag away from you a short distance. As it returns, strike the bag with your fist or an open hand. Repeat for the desired number of repetitions.

Don't push the bag too far away from you initially. Too much momentum from the heavy bag will overpower your punch, and can present a risk of injury.

It is also very important not to load up too much on your punches. To get the plyometric effect, the punch should initiate in response to contact with the heavy bag. Wait until you feel the touch of the bag before you move. Loading the punch might make for more impressive sounding punches, but defeats the purpose of the exercise.

Heavy Bag Hits

Fig. 34 — Heavy Bag Hits

Heavy Bag Hits can also be done for different types of punches. For example, you can build better rear hand power by doing hits as if throwing a cross. Always work with small amounts of bag momentum until you become accustomed to a new motion. Be careful!

Heavy Bag Kicks: Thrust Kicks, Roundhouse Kicks

Description

Heavy Bag Kicks employ the same principles of performance as the pushes and hits. These kicks strengthen the hip, leg, and trunk muscles responsible for powerful roundhouse and thrust kicks.

Execution

Heavy Bag Kicks are best done using thrust kicks and round-house kicks where the heavy bag lands above the knee. Doing roundhouses with contact below the knee puts a dangerous amount of stress upon the knee joint and ligaments. Don't do heavy bag plyos this way.

Do Thrust Kicks much like Heavy Bag Pushes. Stand on-guard or with your kick leg loaded for a strike. Push the bag away and then thrust explosively at the instant it swings back into your foot.

Fig. 35 — Heavy Bag Thrust Kicks

Roundhouse Kicks are done more like Heavy Bag Hits. Use less swing of the heavy bag and less loading of the kick leg. You should feel as if you are "popping" the bag repeatedly off your thigh. Be careful not to injure your hip-flexor muscles by using too much heavy bag momentum.

Fig. 36 —Heavy Bag Roundhouse Kicks

❖   ❖   ❖

THE ROUTINES

In the last chapter, we covered a variety of plyometric exercises. But simply knowing a bunch of plyos is not enough. The key to optimum gains is an intelligently planned, properly executed *progression* of training—that's the purpose of the routines in this chapter. They will move you at the optimum pace along the path to maximum explosive power.

In addition to the basic **Explosive Power** routine, you'll also find special routines for specific needs. Bodybuilders will find a new, experimental routine we believe represents a revolution in the optimum approach to muscular development. Martial artists will discover how plyometric exercise using a heavy bag can make an immediate and significant improvement in punching and kicking power.

And, of course, no matter what sport you play—from weekend racquetball to professional soccer—you can use any of the plyometric routines in **Explosive Power** to promote superior speed-strength.

OPTIMUM EXERCISE SEQUENCE

Successful strength training and muscle-building programs rely on the right sequence of exercises. Other *Health For Life* courses, such as **Secrets of Advanced Bodybuilders**, stress the importance of **proper exercise sequence** for developing muscle mass. One example is the recommendation to do functional strength exercises (those involving many muscles acting together; e.g., Squats, Bench Press, Bent-Over Rows) *before* isolation exercises (those that mainly involve the target muscle; e.g., Lateral Flyes, Triceps Kick-Backs).

Effective plyometric training also depends on proper sequencing of exercises. Here are the rules:

- **Rhythm plyos** should be done first. Rhythm drills prepare your neuro-muscular system for the intensity of speed and power exercises. They also serve as part of your warm-up, helping to decrease risk of injury.

- **Speed plyos** should be done next. The neuro-muscular intensity of these exercises requires the muscles to be thoroughly warmed up, but fresh. Fatigue inhibits your training for maximum speed, so you do these exercises before power training.

- **Power plyos** should be done last because they're the most exhausting. Like speed plyos, power plyos are quite intense—but unlike speed plyos, they incorporate a tremendous application of force. With certain power drills, your muscles will experience a strain equal to many times your bodyweight! As a consequence, power plyos give your body quite a workout even though you may not always feel especially tired. Always do power work last.

PICKING THE RIGHT STARTING LEVEL

There are seven levels to the basic *Explosive Power* routine, progressing from beginning to very advanced.

Lettered levels, such as *Level A*, are intended as a starting point for those with little athletic experience. Use them if you haven't done plyometric training before, or have minimum weight training experience or poor coordination.

Actually, it's a good idea for *everyone* to start at *Level A*. Even if you have good strength and are familiar with plyometric training, you will benefit from a gradual reintroduction. Moreover, starting out easy will help prevent injuries by allowing you to get reaccustomed to the intense eccentric loading of the muscles.

Numbered levels, such as *Level 1*, are the jumping off point for serious training. If you have done plyometric training before and have good upper- and lower-body strength, you may want to start right out with the *Level 1* routine. Remember, though, that while plyometrics often *seem* easy and non-demanding, *they're not.* They put tremendous stress on your body even though they don't give you the immediate burn you get from weight training. So think seriously before starting right out on *Level 1.*

You may find you'd like to do different level routines for upper and lower body. There's no problem with that. Often, the strength and ballistic capacities of these halves of the body are unbalanced. While we recommend striving for overall development, it is acceptable to split the routines along the way.

When To Change Levels

When you can do the exercises on a given level easily, with good technique and at high intensity—*and you have ceased to make progress*—that's the time to move to the next level. As long as you continue to improve, stay on the same level. Making progress means that you are working at an appropriate overload. Rushing ahead only makes you work harder than necessary for the same gains.

MEASURING YOUR PROGRESS

Measuring progress in certain athletic activities is easy. In weightlifting, for instance, you just look for greater maximum strength and increased muscle mass.

Measuring progress from plyometric training is somewhat more complex. The clearest measure of speed-strength progress is sports performance. Are you jumping higher? Are your kicks more powerful? Are you hitting and throwing with greater power? Can you run faster? These are the true measures of explosive power.

There are some simple objective measures that you can use to assess your progress, though. First, though you may not gain much weight from plyometric training, you should become stronger. As your maximum strength improves, your max for functional strength exercises should rise. Second, you should perform better on tests of athletic power. Your vertical jump, standing long jump or triple jump, time for a 30-meter sprint, or distance for multiple bounds are all good measures of explosive leg strength. Throwing a medicine ball for distance, timed weight lifts, and Power Push-Ups for reps or time are all good measures of explosive upper-body strength.

To track your progress accurately, establish a baseline by testing yourself before you begin the **Explosive Power** program, then retest at regular intervals afterward. Use the tests mentioned above or devise a test specific to your individual sport or athletic goals. For example: martial artists may want to see how many roundhouse kicks they can deliver in 5 to 10 seconds as a measure of kicking speed-strength; bodybuilders may want to record maxes for Bench Press, Lying French Press, Close-Grip Pull-Downs, and Squats, or simply take measurements of major bodyparts.

WARMING UP

The intense, explosive nature of plyometric training puts great stress on muscles, joints and connective tissue, making warming-up before a plyometric workout *mandatory*. Failing to warm-up before plyo training all but guarantees injury; doing a warm-up makes muscle tissue more pliable and responsive to stress, decreasing risk of injury.

Your warm-up must accomplish three things. It must:

- raise both your core and target-muscle temperature by about a degree and a half, or enough to bring on a light sweat
- prepare the specific muscles involved for the movement patterns to come
- loosen up the target muscles to prevent muscle tightness from interfering with exercise execution and increasing risk of injury.

The best way to meet the first requirement is with 5 to 10 minutes of easy aerobic running or cycling. The best way to meet the second is by walking quickly through all the movements in the upcoming plyo workout in an non-plyometric way—do medicine ball drills without the medicine ball, do jumping drills with a tiny hop, instead of a full jump, and so on. And the best way to accomplish the third is by *light* stretching.

Keep in mind that when you stretch during a warm-up, you should not work to increase flexibility, but simply to "make available" the full range of motion developed during *prior* flexibility training. This is called **mobility training**—gentle movement that gets your body ready for strenuous exercise. (The best time to work to *increase* flexibility is at the end of your workout, not the beginning. Muscles are fully warmed up and fatigued at that point, making stretching more productive, less tiring, and considerably less painful.)

One final point. If your plyos follow some other part of your workout, perhaps a less demanding one, always make sure that you are still fully warmed up and ready before beginning the plyo drills.

ALLOWING ADEQUATE REST

Plyometric training requires more rest than conventional strength training or bodybuilding because building power through total explosive movement demands that the target muscles be rested prior to each exercise. To put that in terms of *Health For Life's* **fatigue/tension principle,*** it's *not* appropriate to strive for a high fatigue-tension level during a plyometric workout.

Between Sets

Experts recommend different rest times between sets, but the generally accepted guideline is to rest 10 times as long as it takes to do a set. So, for example, if one set of an exercise takes 10 seconds, you should rest 100 seconds (1½ to 2 minutes) between sets. If anything, err on the side of too much rest. Too little rest decreases the effectiveness of your workout and dramatically increases your risk of injury.

Between Exercises

Between exercises, take somewhat more rest. About 3 to 5 minutes works well. This will often seem like far too much time, but keep in mind that you should feel little overall fatigue during the workout itself. It's very difficult to be explosive when you're tired and out of breath.

During Plyotonic Training

One exception to this rule: If you are doing the special *plyotonic* program for bodybuilders (which we'll describe in a moment), rests should be kept short to elevate fatigue-tension levels, a requirement for optimum muscle growth. We'll discuss these rest periods when we cover the program itself.

---

*The fatigue/tension principle reflects the interaction between *fatigue* (determined by weight lifted, number of reps and sets, and rest length) and *tension* (determined by weight lifted). See any of *Health For Life's* resistance training course for details.

Always keep in mind that good plyometric technique is vital for achieving maximum progress with minimum risk of injury. Read the exercise descriptions and study the illustrations carefully.

Note: Where a routine calls for Butt Kicks, you may choose whether to do version 1 or 2 (see page 33).

LOWER BODY

2 sets	Rhythm Skips	30 meters
2 sets	Ankle Bounces	10 reps
2 sets	High-Knee Runs	20 meters
2 sets	Butt Kicks	20 meters
2 sets	Two-Leg Power Hops (w/mini hop)	10 reps

UPPER BODY

2 sets	Medicine Ball Push Passes	10 reps
2 sets	Medicine Ball Twist Tosses	10 reps
2 sets	Kneeling Power Push-Ups	8 reps

LOWER BODY

2 sets	Rhythm Skips	40 meters
2 sets	Ankle Bounces	15 reps
2 sets	High-Knee Runs	20 meters
2 sets	Butt Kicks	20 meters
2 sets	Rhythm Bounds	20 meters
2 sets	Two-Leg Power Hops (w/mini hop)	10 reps
2 sets	Power Skips	20 meters

UPPER BODY

3 sets	Medicine Ball Push Passes	8 reps
3 sets	Medicine Ball Twist Tosses	8 reps
3 sets	Kneeling Power Push-Ups	8 reps

USING GOOD TECHNIQUE

THE BASIC EXPLOSIVE POWER ROUTINE

Level A

Level B

Level 1

LOWER BODY

2 sets .... Rhythm Skips .... 30 meters
2 sets .... Ankle Bounces .... 15 reps
2 sets .... High-Knee Runs .... 20 meters
2 sets .... Butt Kicks .... 20 meters
2 sets .... Speed Skips .... 20 meters
2 sets .... Power Skips .... 20 meters
2 sets .... Two-Leg Power Hops .... 10 reps

UPPER BODY

2 sets .... Medicine Ball Push Passes .... 10 reps
2 sets .... Medicine Ball Twist Tosses .... 10 reps
2 sets .... Medicine Ball Standing Overhead Tosses .... 10 reps
3 sets .... Kneeling Power Push-Ups .... 8 reps

Level 2

LOWER BODY

2 sets .... High-Knee Runs .... 20 meters
2 sets .... Butt Kicks .... 20 meters
2 sets .... Speed Skips .... 20 meters
2 sets .... Speed Hops .... 10 reps
2 sets .... Power Skips .... 20 meters
2 sets .... Power Bounds .... 20 meters
2 sets .... Two-Leg Side Hops .... 8 reps

UPPER BODY

3 sets .... Medicine Ball Push Passes .... 8 reps
3 sets .... Medicine Ball Twist Tosses .... 8 reps
3 sets .... Medicine Ball Standing Overhead Tosses .... 8 reps
2 sets .... Power Push-Ups .... 6 reps

Level 3

LOWER BODY

2 sets .... Jumping Rope (fast pace) .... 30 seconds
2 sets .... Rhythm Skips .... 30 meters
2 sets .... Speed Skips .... 20 meters
3 sets .... Speed Hops .... 10 reps
2 sets .... Power Skips .... 20 meters
2 sets .... Power Bounds .... 20 meters
2 sets .... Two-Leg Power Hops .... 6 reps
2 sets .... Two-Leg Side Hops .... 6 reps

UPPER BODY

3 sets .... Medicine Ball Push Passes .... 8 reps
3 sets .... Medicine Ball Twist Tosses .... 8 reps
3 sets .... Medicine Ball Standing Overhead Tosses .... 8 reps
3 sets .... Power Push-Ups .... 6 reps

Level 4

LOWER BODY

3 sets .... Jumping Rope (fast pace) .... 25 seconds
2 sets ...... Skip Kicks .... 20 meters
2 sets ...... Speed Skips .... 20 meters
3 sets ...... Speed Hops .... 10 reps
4 sets ...... Assisted Sprints .... 40 meters
3 sets ...... Power Bounds .... 20 meters
2 sets ...... One-Leg Hops .... 6 reps @ leg
2 sets ...... Alternate-Leg Side Hops .... 6 reps

UPPER BODY

3 sets .... Medicine Ball Push Passes .... 8 reps
3 sets .... Medicine Ball Twist Tosses .... 8 reps
3 sets .... Medicine Ball Kneeling Overhead Tosses .... 8 reps
4 sets .... Power Push-Ups .... 6 reps

Level 5

LOWER BODY

3 sets .... Jumping Rope (fast pace) .... 25 seconds
2 sets ...... Skip Kicks .... 20 meters
2 sets ...... Speed Skips .... 20 meters
3 sets ...... Speed Hops .... 10 reps
5 sets ...... Assisted Sprints .... 50 to 60 meters
3 sets ...... Power Bounds .... 30 meters
3 sets ...... One-Leg Hops .... 6 reps @ leg
2 sets ...... Box Jumps (12"-18" platform) .... 5 reps

UPPER BODY

3 sets .... Medicine Ball Push Passes .... 10 reps
3 sets .... Medicine Ball Twist Tosses .... 10 reps
3 sets .... Medicine Ball Kneeling Overhead Tosses ..... 10 reps
4 sets .... Power Push-Ups .... 8 reps

The beauty of plyometric training is in the specificity and variation it can encompass. Learn to adapt your training to your specific needs. If you use a lot of side-to-side movement in your sport, substitute extra lateral motion exercises in place of linear ones. If all your activity is power-related, deemphasize the speed component of your training.

Almost any movement can be done plyometrically. Turning the specific movements of your sport into a plyometric conditioning exercise will lead to greater explosive power!

EXPLOSIVE POWER TRAINING FOR MARTIAL ARTISTS

The *Basic Explosive Power Routine* will help martial artists add greater force and speed to their kicks and hand-strikes. But the following modified version below takes you further, faster, by incorporating heavy bag drills that closely imitate movements used in martial arts.

For your convenience, the basic *Level A* and *B* routines are duplicated below; the martial-arts-specific exercises start on *Level 1*.

Level A

LOWER BODY

2 sets ....Rhythm Skips...30 meters
2 sets ....Ankle Bounces ....10 reps
2 sets ....High-Knee Runs .... 20 meters
2 sets ....Butt Kicks.. 20 meters
2 sets ....Two-Leg Power Hops (w/mini hop).................10 reps

UPPER BODY

2 sets ....Medicine Ball Push Passes....................................10 reps
2 sets ....Medicine Ball Twist Tosses ....10 reps
2 sets ....Kneeling Power Push-Ups ....8 reps

Level B

LOWER BODY

2 sets ....Rhythm Skips..................................... 40 meters
2 sets ....Ankle Bounces ....15 reps
2 sets ....High-Knee Runs .... 20 meters
2 sets ....Butt Kicks.. 20 meters
2 sets ....Rhythm Bounds.. 20 meters
2 sets ....Two-Leg Power Hops (w/mini hop) ....10 reps
2 sets ....Power Skips... 20 meters

UPPER BODY

3 sets .... Medicine Ball Push Passes .... 8 reps
3 sets .... Medicine Ball Twist Tosses .... 8 reps
3 sets .... Kneeling Power Push-Ups .... 8 reps

LOWER BODY

2 sets .... Rhythm Skips ....30 meters
2 sets .... Ankle Bounces .... 15 reps
2 sets .... High-Knee Runs ....20 meters
2 sets .... Butt Kicks ....20 meters
2 sets .... Speed Skips .... 20 meters
2 sets .... Power Skips ....20 meters
2 sets .... Heavy Bag Thrust Kicks .... 8-10 reps @ leg

UPPER BODY

3 sets .... Heavy Bag Pushes ....6-8 reps
2 sets .... Medicine Ball Twist Tosses .... 10 reps
2 sets .... Medicine Ball Standing Overhead Tosses ..... 10 reps
3 sets .... Kneeling Power Push-Ups .... 8 reps

LOWER BODY

2 sets .... High-Knee Runs ....20 meters
2 sets .... Butt Kicks ....20 meters
2 sets .... Speed Skips ....20 meters
2 sets .... Speed Hops .... 10 reps
2 sets .... Power Skips ....20 meters
3 sets .... Heavy Bag Thrust Kicks ....6-8 reps @ leg
2 sets .... Two-Leg Side Hops .... 8 reps

UPPER BODY

3 sets .... Heavy Bag Pushes ....6-8 reps
3 sets .... Medicine Ball Twist Tosses .... 8 reps
3 sets .... Medicine Ball Standing Overhead Tosses .... 8 reps
3 sets .... Kneeling Power Push-Ups .... 6 reps

LOWER BODY

2 sets .... Jumping Rope (fast pace) ....30 seconds
2 sets .... Rhythm Skips ....30 meters
2 sets .... Speed Skips .... 20 meters
3 sets .... Speed Hops .... 10 reps

Level 1

Level 2

Level 3

2 sets ....Power Skips...20 meters
2 sets ....Heavy Bag Thrust Kicks ....6 reps @ leg
2 sets ....Heavy Bag Roundhouse Kicks ....8 reps @ leg
2 sets ....Two-Leg Side Hops ....6 reps

UPPER BODY

3 sets ....Heavy Bag Hits... 6-8 reps @ side
3 sets ....Medicine Ball Twist Tosses ....8 reps
3 sets ....Medicine Ball Standing Overhead Tosses ....8 reps
3 sets ....Kneeling Power Push-Ups ....6 reps

Level 4

LOWER BODY

3 sets ....Jumping Rope (fast pace) ....25 seconds
2 sets ....Skipping Kicks .... 20 meters
2 sets ....Speed Skips .... 20 meters
3 sets ....Speed Hops ....10 reps
3 sets ....Heavy Bag Roundhouse Kicks ....6 reps @ leg
3 sets ....Heavy Bag Thrust Kicks ....8 reps @ leg
2 sets ....One-Leg Hops...6 reps @ leg
2 sets ....Alternate-Leg Side Hops ....6 reps

UPPER BODY

2 sets ....Heavy Bag Pushes.....................................8-10 reps
3 sets ....Medicine Ball Twist Tosses ....8 reps
3 sets ....Heavy Bag Hits...8 reps @ side
2 sets ....Power Push-Ups..6 reps

Level 5

LOWER BODY

3 sets ....Jumping Rope (fast pace) ....25 seconds
2 sets ....Skipping Kicks .... 20 meters
2 sets ....Speed Skips .... 20 meters
3 sets ....Speed Hops ....10 reps
3 sets ....Heavy Bag Roundhouse Kicks ....6-8 @ leg
3 sets ....Power Bounds..30 meters
3 sets ....One-Leg Hops...6 reps @ leg
3 sets ....Heavy Bag Thrust Kicks ....8-10 reps @ leg

UPPER BODY

2 sets ....Heavy Bag Pushes.....................................6-8 reps
3 sets ....Heavy Bag Hits... 6-8 reps @ side
3 sets ....Medicine Ball Twist Tosses ....10 reps
3 sets ....Medicine Ball Kneeling Overhead Tosses..........10 reps
2 sets ....Power Push-Ups..8 reps

PLYOTONIC TRAINING FOR BODYBUILDERS

In Chapter 1, we explained how plyometric work can help bodybuilders train at a higher intensity by increasing voluntary activation capacity. Just adding one or two short plyometric sessions per week in addition to conventional lifting workouts should allow you to take advantage of this benefit.

But plyos may offer the bodybuilder even more. Developments in strength training theory suggest that doing plyometric training and weight lifting *within the same training session* may create a synergistic effect *far* beyond that of weight training alone or a more conventional arrangement of plyometric sessions plus weight training sessions.

HFL has developed a special new training regimen to maximize the potential synergy between plyometrics and conventional (isotonic) weight training. This approach, which we call **plyotonic training**, is simple: You precede the group of exercises for a particular bodypart with a single plyometric exercise that targets that same bodypart. This "preconditions" the target muscle for greater gains in two—and possibly three—ways:

■ First, it increases fiber recruitment as explained in Chapter 1. As a result, when you lift, a greater percentage of muscle fibers actually get trained. Greater activation translates into increased exercise intensity.

■ Second, even beyond the greater *voluntary* activation that results from plyo work, you get greater overall activation. That's because the eccentric contractions during plyo exercises themselves activate an additional percentage of fibers that cannot be recruited voluntarily.

■ Third—and this is speculative—doing plyometrics immediately prior to a lift may in effect temporarily lower your absolute strength level with relatively less effect on your maximum strength level. This may cause the target muscle to "perceive" the resistance as representing a greater overload than it would under normal circumstances, increasing the potential for growth.

The bottom line is that this type of combined training allows you to work with greater intensity using more of your total muscle capacity. And that, theoretically, translates into greater gains without overtraining.

The following plyotonic training plan for bodybuilders is new and experimental. We know plyos work for strength development, and we strongly believe that combining plyometric training with conventional weightlifting holds tremendous promise for the future of mass training as well.

Level 1

Do a thorough warm-up, then complete the following short, plyometric session prior to starting your weight routine:

BEFORE LOWER BODY

2 sets	Rhythm Bounds	20 meters
2 sets	Two-Leg Power Hops	8 reps
2 sets	Ankle Bounces	12 reps

BEFORE UPPER BODY

1 set	Medicine Ball Push Passes	8 reps
1 set	Medicine Ball Twist Tosses	8 reps
1 set	Medicine Ball Standing Overhead Tosses	8 reps
1 set	Kneeling Power Push-Ups	5 reps

During the weightlifting workout itself,* do one set of an appropriate exercise between each functional strength exercise or superset of the weight training routine. The total number of sets during the weight training routine should not exceed six for the entire body.

EXAMPLE: STARTING UPPER BODY / WORKING CHEST

1 set	Upper-Body Plyo Series (from routine above)	
	rest 3-5 minutes	
1 set	Power Push-Ups	5-8 reps
	no rest	
3 sets	Supine Bench Press	6-8 reps
	rest 45-75 sec. between sets	
3 sets	Incline Bench Press	6-8 reps
	rest 45-75 sec. between sets	

Level 2

Do a thorough warm-up, then complete the following short, plyometric session prior to starting your weight routine:

---

*For a complete program of synergistic weight routines for the whole body, see *HFL's* Secrets of Advanced Bodybuilders.

BEFORE LOWER BODY

2 sets .... Rhythm Bounds .... 20 meters
2 sets .... Speed Hops .... 8 reps
2 sets .... Two-Leg Power Hops .... 8 reps
2 sets .... Ankle Bounces .... 12 reps

BEFORE UPPER BODY

2 sets .... Medicine Ball Push Passes .... 8 reps
2 sets .... Medicine Ball Twist Tosses .... 8 reps
2 sets .... Medicine Ball Standing Overhead Tosses .... 8 reps
1 set .... Kneeling Power Push-Ups .... 6-8 reps

Include one set of an appropriate exercise between each functional strength lift or superset. For example, do Two-Leg Power Hops prior to Squats. Your total plyometric sets during the weightlifting routine should not exceed eight.

Level 3

Do a thorough warm-up, then complete the following short, plyometric session prior to the starting your weight routine:

BEFORE LOWER BODY

2 sets .... Speed Hops .... 8 reps
2 sets .... Two-Leg Power Hops .... 8 reps
2 sets .... One-Leg Hops .... 6-8 reps
2 sets .... Ankle Bounces .... 15 reps

BEFORE UPPER BODY

3 sets .... Medicine Ball Push Passes .... 6-8 reps
2 sets .... Medicine Ball Twist Tosses .... 6-8 reps
2 sets .... Medicine Ball Kneeling Overhead Tosses .... 6-8 reps
2 sets .... Kneeling Power Push-Ups .... 6-8 reps

Include one set of an appropriate plyo exercise between each functional strength weight exercise or superset. Then, for each lift, do one set of five to eight reps at 50% of your rep max, emphasizing dynamic eccentric movement. For example, prior to Lat Pulls do one set of Medicine Ball Overhead Tosses followed by one set of half-weight Lat Pulls with dynamic movement.

The Basic Explosive Power Routines, Lower Body

Illustrated

	RHYTHM SKIPS	ANKLE BOUNCES	HIGH-KNEE RUNS
LEVEL A	2 sets / 30 meters	2 sets / 10 reps	2 sets / 20 meters
LEVEL B	2 sets / 40 meters	2 sets / 15 reps	2 sets / 20 meters

RHYTHM BOUNDS

2 sets / 20 meters

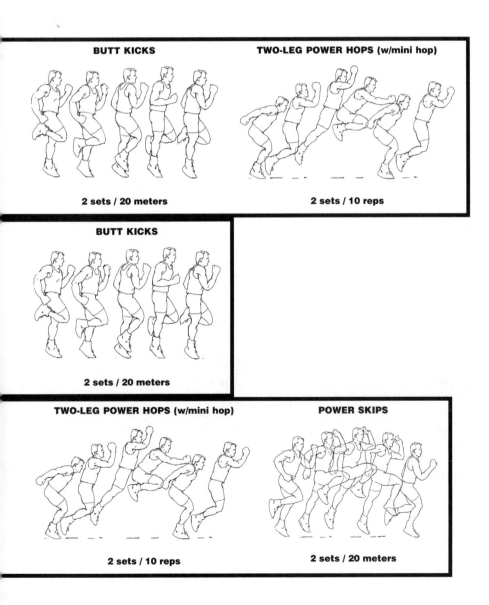

BUTT KICKS

TWO-LEG POWER HOPS (w/mini hop)

2 sets / 20 meters

2 sets / 10 reps

BUTT KICKS

2 sets / 20 meters

TWO-LEG POWER HOPS (w/mini hop)

POWER SKIPS

2 sets / 10 reps

2 sets / 20 meters

79

LEVEL 1

RHYTHM SKIPS

2 sets / 30 meters

ANKLE BOUNCES

2 sets / 15 reps

HIGH-KNEE RUNS

2 sets / 20 meters

SPEED SKIPS

2 sets / 20 meters

LEVEL 2

HIGH-KNEE RUNS

2 sets / 20 meters

BUTT KICKS

2 sets / 20 meters

SPEED HOPS

2 sets / 10 reps

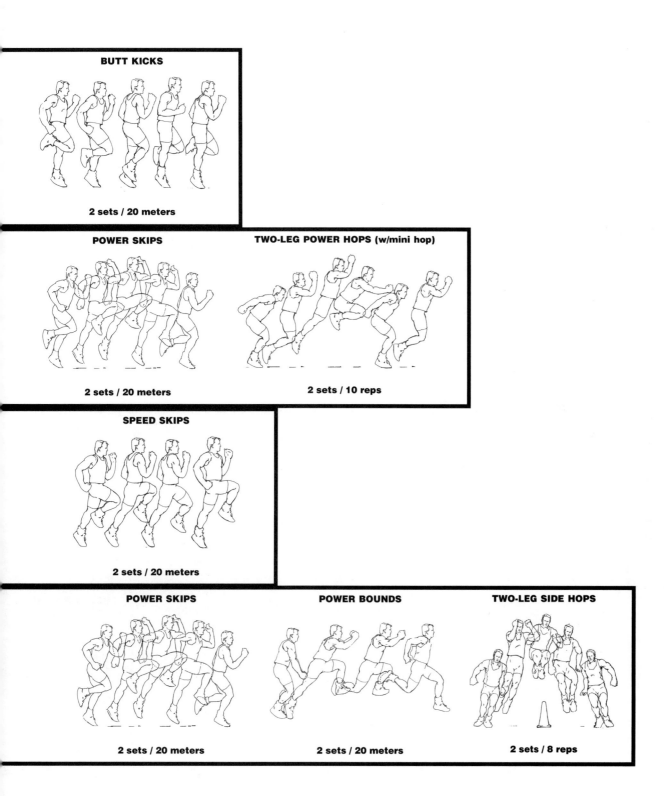

BUTT KICKS

2 sets / 20 meters

POWER SKIPS

2 sets / 20 meters

TWO-LEG POWER HOPS (w/mini hop)

2 sets / 10 reps

SPEED SKIPS

2 sets / 20 meters

POWER SKIPS

2 sets / 20 meters

POWER BOUNDS

2 sets / 20 meters

TWO-LEG SIDE HOPS

2 sets / 8 reps

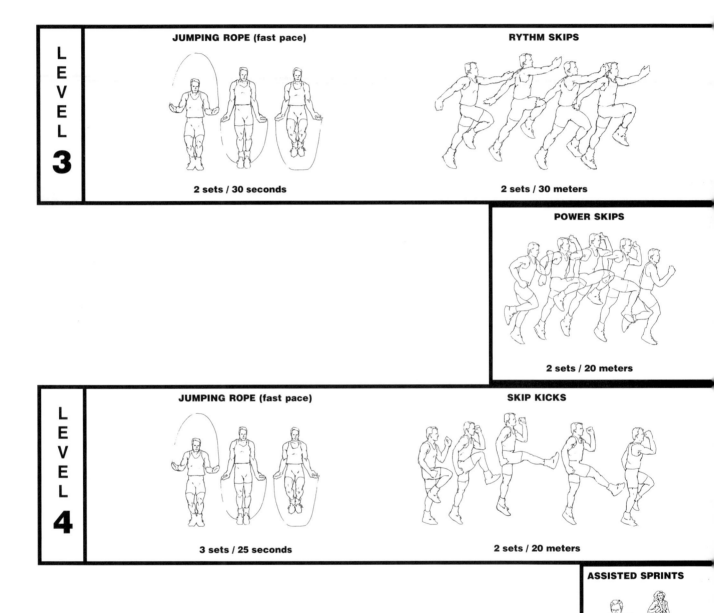

LEVEL 3

JUMPING ROPE (fast pace)

2 sets / 30 seconds

RYTHM SKIPS

2 sets / 30 meters

POWER SKIPS

2 sets / 20 meters

LEVEL 4

JUMPING ROPE (fast pace)

3 sets / 25 seconds

SKIP KICKS

2 sets / 20 meters

ASSISTED SPRINTS

4 sets / 40 meters

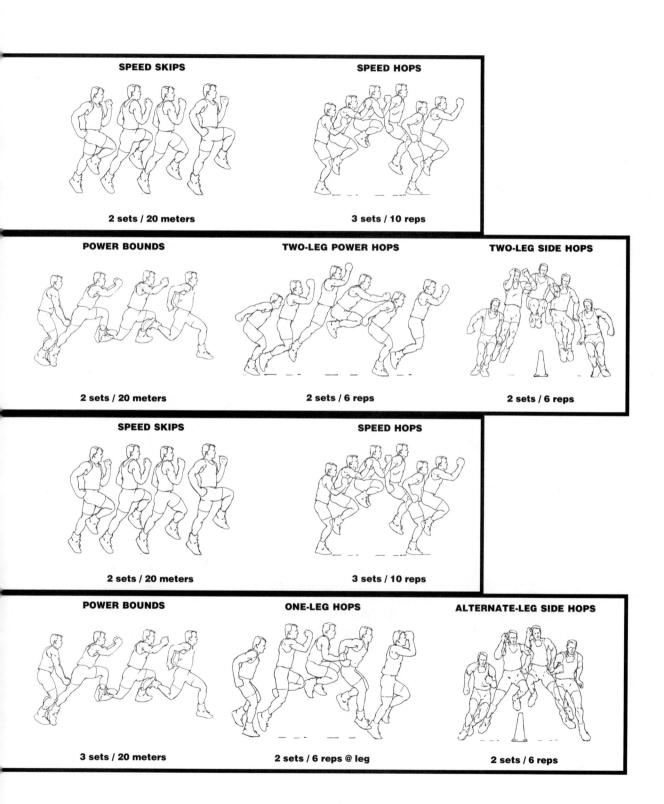

SPEED SKIPS

2 sets / 20 meters

SPEED HOPS

3 sets / 10 reps

POWER BOUNDS

2 sets / 20 meters

TWO-LEG POWER HOPS

2 sets / 6 reps

TWO-LEG SIDE HOPS

2 sets / 6 reps

SPEED SKIPS

2 sets / 20 meters

SPEED HOPS

3 sets / 10 reps

POWER BOUNDS

3 sets / 20 meters

ONE-LEG HOPS

2 sets / 6 reps @ leg

ALTERNATE-LEG SIDE HOPS

2 sets / 6 reps

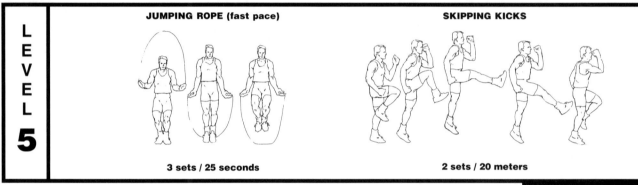

LEVEL 5

JUMPING ROPE (fast pace)

3 sets / 25 seconds

SKIPPING KICKS

2 sets / 20 meters

ASSISTED SPRINTS

5 sets / 50 to 60 meters

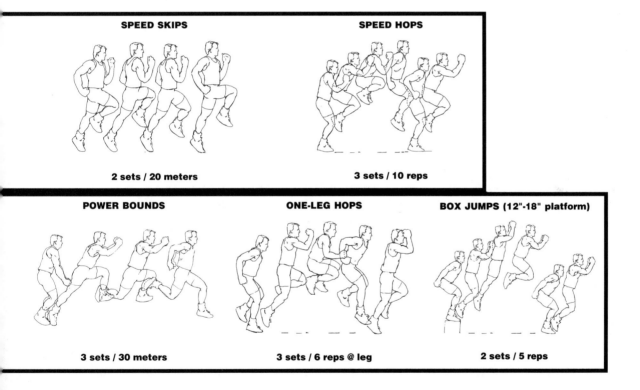

SPEED SKIPS

2 sets / 20 meters

SPEED HOPS

3 sets / 10 reps

POWER BOUNDS

3 sets / 30 meters

ONE-LEG HOPS

3 sets / 6 reps @ leg

BOX JUMPS (12"-18" platform)

2 sets / 5 reps

	MEDICINE BALL PUSH PASSES	MEDICINE BALL TWIST TOSSES
LEVEL A	2 sets / 10 reps	2 sets / 10 reps
LEVEL B	3 sets / 8 reps	3 sets / 8 reps
LEVEL 1	2 sets / 10 reps	2 sets / 10 reps

The Basic Explosive Power Routines, Upper Body

Illustrated

KNEELING POWER PUSH-UPS

2 sets / 8 reps

KNEELING POWER PUSH-UPS

3 sets / 8 reps

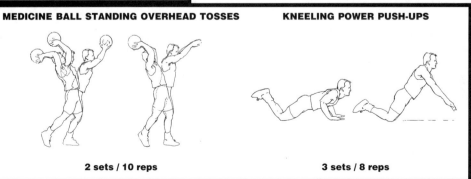

MEDICINE BALL STANDING OVERHEAD TOSSES

2 sets / 10 reps

KNEELING POWER PUSH-UPS

3 sets / 8 reps

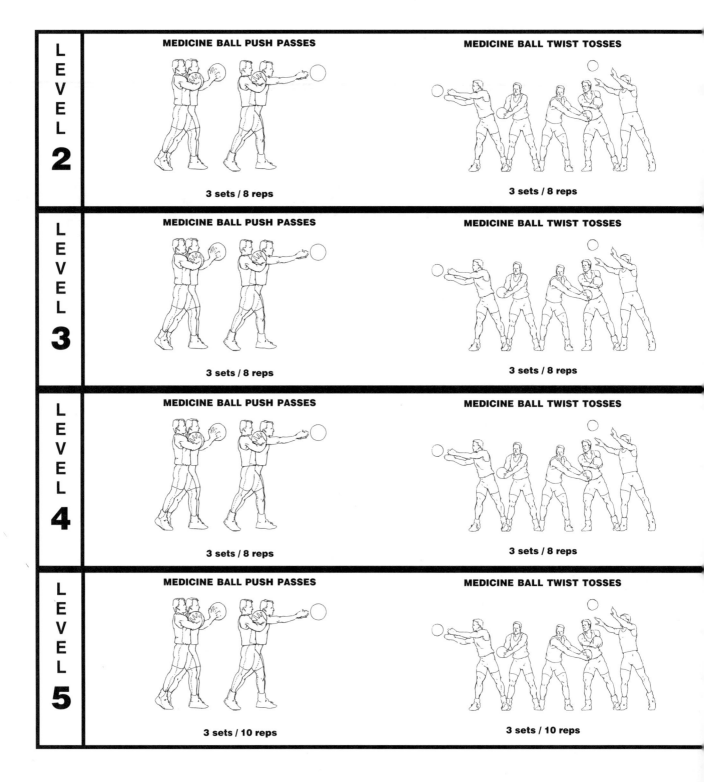

	MEDICINE BALL PUSH PASSES	MEDICINE BALL TWIST TOSSES
LEVEL 2	3 sets / 8 reps	3 sets / 8 reps
LEVEL 3	3 sets / 8 reps	3 sets / 8 reps
LEVEL 4	3 sets / 8 reps	3 sets / 8 reps
LEVEL 5	3 sets / 10 reps	3 sets / 10 reps

MEDICINE BALL STANDING OVERHEAD TOSSES

POWER PUSH-UPS

3 sets / 8 reps

2 sets / 6 reps

MEDICINE BALL STANDING OVERHEAD TOSSES

POWER PUSH-UPS

3 sets / 8 reps

3 sets / 6 reps

MEDICINE BALL KNEELING OVERHEAD TOSSES

POWER PUSH-UPS

3 sets / 8 reps

4 sets / 6 reps

MEDICINE BALL KNEELING OVERHEAD TOSSES

POWER PUSH-UPS

3 sets / 10 reps

4 sets / 8 reps

Explosive Power Training for Martial Artists, Lower Body

Illustrated

	RHYTHM SKIPS	ANKLE BOUNCES	HIGH-KNEE RUNS
LEVEL A	2 sets / 30 meters	2 sets / 10 reps	2 sets / 20 meters
LEVEL B	2 sets / 40 meters	2 sets / 15 reps	2 sets / 20 meters

RHYTHM BOUNDS

2 sets / 20 meters

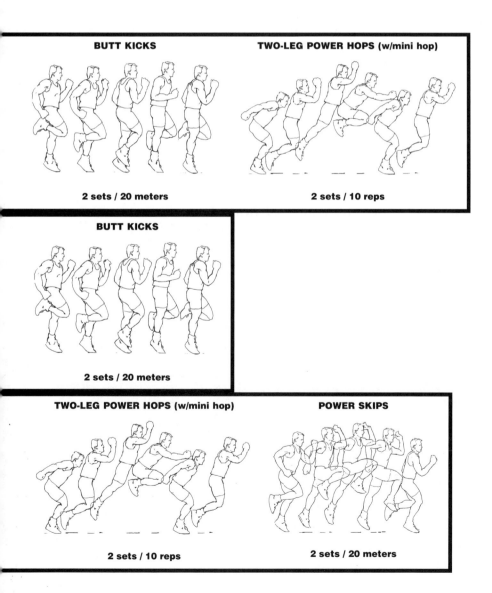

BUTT KICKS

2 sets / 20 meters

TWO-LEG POWER HOPS (w/mini hop)

2 sets / 10 reps

BUTT KICKS

2 sets / 20 meters

TWO-LEG POWER HOPS (w/mini hop)

2 sets / 10 reps

POWER SKIPS

2 sets / 20 meters

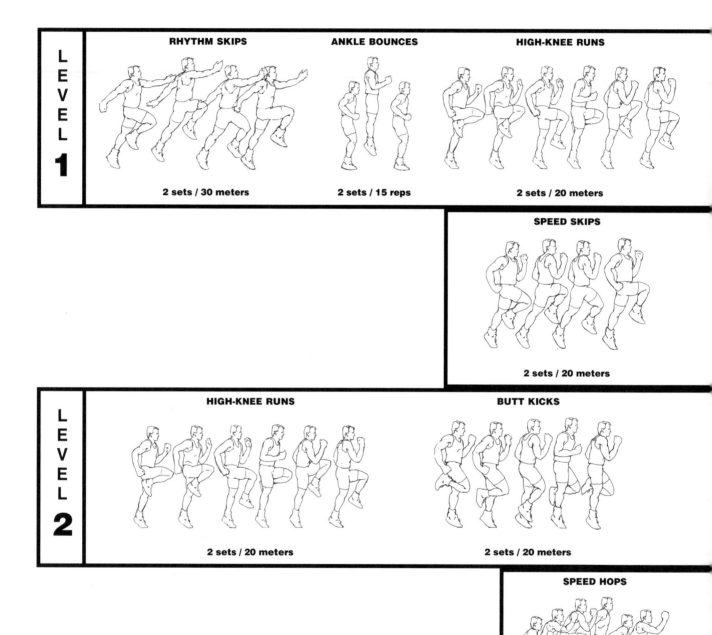

LEVEL 1

RHYTHM SKIPS

2 sets / 30 meters

ANKLE BOUNCES

2 sets / 15 reps

HIGH-KNEE RUNS

2 sets / 20 meters

SPEED SKIPS

2 sets / 20 meters

LEVEL 2

HIGH-KNEE RUNS

2 sets / 20 meters

BUTT KICKS

2 sets / 20 meters

SPEED HOPS

2 sets / 10 reps

BUTT KICKS

2 sets / 20 meters

POWER SKIPS

2 sets / 20 meters

HEAVY BAG THRUST KICKS

2 sets / 8-10 reps @ leg

SPEED SKIPS

2 sets / 20 meters

POWER SKIPS

2 sets / 20 meters

HEAVY BAG THRUST KICKS

3 sets / 6-8 reps @ leg

TWO-LEG SIDE HOPS

2 sets / 8 reps

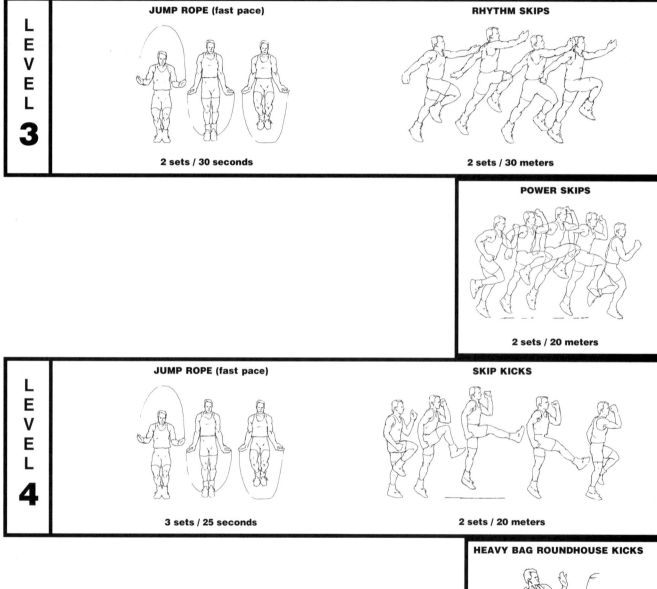

LEVEL 3

JUMP ROPE (fast pace)

2 sets / 30 seconds

RHYTHM SKIPS

2 sets / 30 meters

POWER SKIPS

2 sets / 20 meters

LEVEL 4

JUMP ROPE (fast pace)

3 sets / 25 seconds

SKIP KICKS

2 sets / 20 meters

HEAVY BAG ROUNDHOUSE KICKS

3 sets / 6 reps @ leg

SPEED SKIPS

2 sets / 20 meters

SPEED HOPS

3 sets / 10 reps

HEAVY BAG THRUST KICKS

2 sets / 6 reps @ leg

HEAVY BAG ROUNDHOUSE KICKS

2 sets / 8 reps @ leg

TWO-LEG SIDE HOPS

2 sets / 6 reps

SPEED SKIPS

2 sets / 20 meters

SPEED HOPS

3 sets / 10 reps

HEAVY BAG THRUST KICKS

3 sets / 8 reps @ leg

ONE-LEG HOPS

2 sets / 6 reps @ leg

ALTERNATE-LEG SIDE HOPS

2 sets / 6 reps

L
E
V
E
L
5

JUMP ROPE (fast pace)

3 sets / 25 seconds

SKIP KICKS

2 sets / 20 meters

HEAVY BAG ROUNDHOUSE KICKS

3 sets / 6-8 reps @ leg

SPEED SKIPS

2 sets / 20 meters

SPEED HOPS

3 sets / 10 reps

POWER BOUNDS

3 sets / 30 meters

ONE-LEG HOPS

3 sets / 6 reps @ leg

HEAVY BAG THRUST KICKS

3 sets / 8-10 reps @ leg

Explosive Power Training for Martial Artists, Upper Body

Illustrated

LEVEL A

MEDICINE BALL PUSH PASSES
2 sets / 10 reps

MEDICINE BALL TWIST TOSSES
2 sets / 10 reps

LEVEL B

MEDICINE BALL PUSH PASSES
3 sets / 8 reps

MEDICINE BALL TWIST TOSSES
3 sets / 8 reps

LEVEL 1

HEAVY BAG PUSHES
3 sets / 6-8 reps

MEDICINE BALL TWIST TOSSES
2 sets / 10 reps

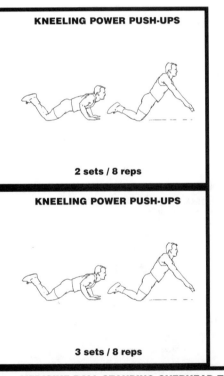

KNEELING POWER PUSH-UPS

2 sets / 8 reps

KNEELING POWER PUSH-UPS

3 sets / 8 reps

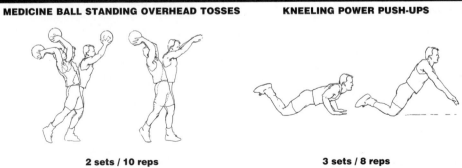

MEDICINE BALL STANDING OVERHEAD TOSSES

2 sets / 10 reps

KNEELING POWER PUSH-UPS

3 sets / 8 reps

LEVEL 2

HEAVY BAG PUSHES
3 sets / 6-8 reps

MEDICINE BALL TWIST TOSSES
3 sets / 8 reps

LEVEL 3

HEAVY BAG HITS
3 sets / 6-8 reps @ side

MEDICINE BALL TWIST TOSSES
3 sets / 8 reps

LEVEL 4

HEAVY BAG PUSHES
2 sets / 8-10 reps

MEDICINE BALL TWIST TOSSES
3 sets / 8 reps

LEVEL 5

HEAVY BAG PUSHES
2 sets / 6-8 reps

HEAVY BAG HITS
3 sets / 6-8 reps @ side

MEDICINE BALL STANDING OVERHEAD TOSSES

3 sets / 8 reps

KNEELING POWER PUSH-UPS

3 sets / 6 reps

MEDICINE BALL STANDING OVERHEAD TOSSES

3 sets / 8 reps

KNEELING POWER PUSH-UPS

3 sets / 6 reps

HEAVY BAG HITS

3 sets / 8 reps @ side

POWER PUSH-UPS

2 sets / 6 reps

MEDICINE BALL TWIST TOSSES

3 sets / 10 reps

**MEDICINE BALL
KNEELING OVERHEAD TOSSES**

3 sets / 10 reps

POWER PUSH-UPS

2 sets / 8 reps

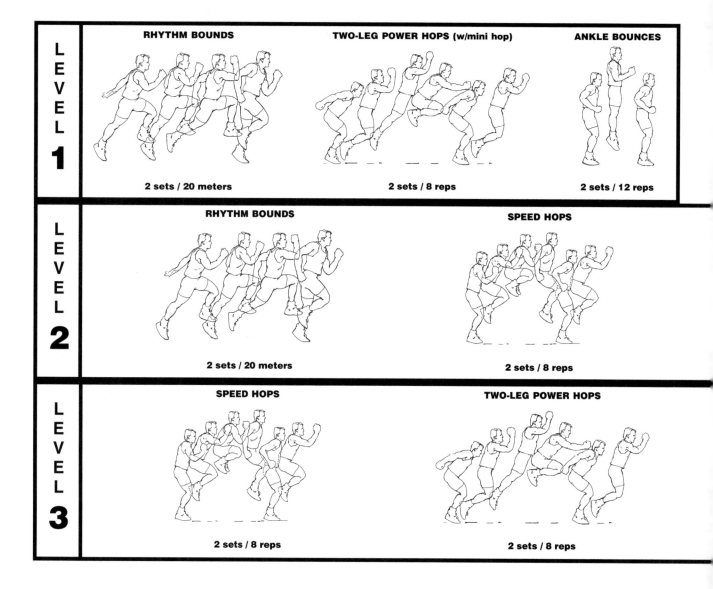

LEVEL 1

RHYTHM BOUNDS

2 sets / 20 meters

TWO-LEG POWER HOPS (w/mini hop)

2 sets / 8 reps

ANKLE BOUNCES

2 sets / 12 reps

LEVEL 2

RHYTHM BOUNDS

2 sets / 20 meters

SPEED HOPS

2 sets / 8 reps

LEVEL 3

SPEED HOPS

2 sets / 8 reps

TWO-LEG POWER HOPS

2 sets / 8 reps

Plyometric Training for Bodybuilders, Before Lower Body
Illustrated

TWO-LEG POWER HOPS
2 sets / 8 reps

ANKLE BOUNCES
2 sets / 12 reps

ONE-LEG HOPS
2 sets / 6-8 reps @ leg

ANKLE BOUNCES
2 sets / 15 reps

LEVEL 1

MEDICINE BALL PUSH PASSES

1 set / 8 reps

MEDICINE BALL TWIST TOSSES

1 set / 8 reps

LEVEL 2

MEDICINE BALL PUSH PASSES

2 sets / 8 reps

MEDICINE BALL TWIST TOSSES

2 sets / 8 reps

LEVEL 3

MEDICINE BALL PUSH PASSES

3 sets / 6-8 reps

MEDICINE BALL TWIST TOSSES

2 sets / 6-8 reps

Plyometric Training for Bodybuilders, Before Upper Body
Illustrated

MEDICINE BALL STANDING OVERHEAD TOSSES

1 set / 8 reps

KNEELING POWER PUSH-UPS

1 set / 5 reps

MEDICINE BALL STANDING OVERHEAD TOSSES

2 sets / 8 reps

KNEELING POWER PUSH-UPS

1 set / 6-8 reps

MEDICINE BALL KNEELING OVERHEAD TOSSES

2 sets / 6-8 reps

KNEELING POWER PUSH-UPS

2 sets / 6-8 reps

THE SCHEDULE

The *Exercises* chapter presented the building blocks out of which we constructed the routines; the *Routines* chapter laid out the training you should do on any given day. Now let's see how you combine those daily routines into a weekly or yearly training schedule.

PLYOMETRIC TRAINING FOR MOST SPORTS

Plyometric training is like salt—a little goes a long way, and adding more beyond what's appropriate does not improve results. In fact, we've already said that because of the intense neuro-muscular overload plyos impose, you need a good 48—and preferably 72—hours of rest between sessions. That means you should use the **Explosive Power** routines a *maximum* of twice per week. Doing plyos *three* times a week will usually leave you too tired to train competently or compete effectively in your sport.

Combining Different Kinds of Training

To integrate the **Explosive Power** routines with your other forms of training, follow these two rules:

■ Do plyo work for your upper body on the same days you do other upper-body conditioning exercises, and plyo work for your lower body on the same days you do other lower-body conditioning exercises. This allows all bodyparts maximum recovery time between workouts.

■ When combining skill work, plyos, and resistance training, always do skill training first, then plyos, then resistance work. You do skill training first because it's hard to train subtle motor control patterns into your nervous system when you're tired—and you *will* be tired if you do either plyos or resistance work first. You do plyometric training next (before the resistance work) because it's safer to do plyos when your muscles aren't tired. And you do resistance training last because of the increased activation facilitated by prior plyo training.

Once again in fewer words: Do the **Explosive Power** routines a maximum of twice per week, allow 48 to 72 hours between sessions, and do similar activities on the same days.

Plyotonic training should also be done no more than twice a week per bodypart. In fact, if you are a beginner, you should limit it to once per week—the first day of that week's training.

Intermediate and advanced athletes should go ahead and do plyotonic training twice per week according to the guidelines below.

If you work your whole body **three times per week,** you should do plyotonics on the *first* and *last* day of training each week. Again, this will give you plenty of recovery time between plyometric sessions.

If you split your training (different bodyparts on different days) using a **four-day, upper/lower split**, do upper-body plyos on both upper-body days, and lower-body plyos on both lower-body days. That way, you'll get a good three days of recovery between the training for each bodypart.

PLYOTONIC TRAINING FOR BODYBUILDERS

Whole Body, 3 Times a Week

Traditional 4-Day Split

EXAMPLES OF OPTIMUM SEQUENCING

If you work your whole body **three times per week,** you should do plyotonics on the *first* and *last* day of training each week.

MONDAY	WEDNESDAY	FRIDAY
Plyotonic Training	Conventional Weight Training	**Plyotonic** Training

If you use a **split routine** (different body parts on different days), try to leave as much time between plyotonic workouts for the same bodyparts as possible.

4-day split — Each body part 2 times per week

MONDAY	TUESDAY	WEDNESDAY	THURSDAY	FRIDAY	SATURDAY
Plyotonic *Lower-Body* Training	**Plyotonic** *Upper-Body* Training	[rest]	**Plyotonic** *Lower-Body* Training	**Plyotonic** *Upper-Body* Training	[rest]

6-day split — Each body part 3 times per week

MONDAY	TUESDAY	WEDNESDAY	THURSDAY	FRIDAY	SATURDAY
Plyotonic *Upper-Body* Training	**Plyotonic** *Lower-Body* Training	Conventional *Upper-Body* Training	Conventional *Lower-Body* Training	**Plyotonic** *Upper-Body* Training	**Plyotonic** *Lower-Body* Training

6-day split — Upper split over 2 days, lower done in 1

MONDAY	TUESDAY	WEDNESDAY	THURSDAY	FRIDAY	SATURDAY
Plyotonic *Lower-Body* Training	**Plyotonic** *Upper-Body* Training	Conventional *Upper-Body* Training	**Plyotonic** *Lower-Body* Training	Conventional *Upper-Body* Training	**Plyotonic** *Upper-Body* Training

Health For Life's 5-Day / 3-Week Cycle

MONDAY	TUESDAY	WEDNESDAY	THURSDAY	FRIDAY	SATURDAY
Plyotonic *Lower-Body* Training	Conventional *Back / Biceps* Training	**Plyotonic** *Chest / Triceps* Training	[rest]	**Plyotonic** *Lower-Body* Training	**Plyotonic** *Back / Biceps* Training
Plyotonic *Chest / Triceps* Training	Conventional *Lower-Body* Training	**Plyotonic** *Back / Biceps* Training	[rest]	**Plyotonic** *Chest / Triceps* Training	**Plyotonic** *Lower-Body* Training
Plyotonic *Back / Biceps* Training	Conventional *Chest / Triceps* Training	**Plyotonic** *Lower-Body* Training	[rest]	**Plyotonic** *Back / Biceps* Training	**Plyotonic** *Chest / Triceps* Training

For a **six-day, upper/lower split**—with the upper and lower bodies worked three days a week each—do plyotonic training only two of those days per bodypart.

For example, assume you work upper body on Monday, Wednesday, and Friday and lower on Tuesday, Thursday, and Saturday. You would do upper-body plyotonic training on the two upper days that allow the most rest between workouts—Monday and Friday. Following the same thinking for lower body, you would do lower-body plyotonic training on Tuesday and Saturday.

Scheduling plyotonics for a six-day split in which the upper body muscles are split over two sessions (for a total of four upper-body and two lower-body workouts per week) is a bit trickier. In that case, to balance plyometric and weight training for the various upper-body muscle groups, you would do upper-body plyotonics on the *first* and *last* upper-body days each week. And you would do plyotonic training on *both* lower-body days.

For example, if you train your upper body on Tuesday-Wednesday and Friday-Saturday, you would do your upper-body plyotonic training on Tuesdays and Saturdays.

Scheduling plyotonics for **HFL's special five-day split*** involves the same kind of thinking as scheduling them for a six-day split with the upper-body split over two sessions. Again, you want to balance plyometric and weight training for the various upper-body muscle groups. Rather than try to spell out all three week's worth of daily routines, we refer you to the chart at left.

**Traditional
Six-Day Split**

**HFL's Five-Day,
Three-Week Cycle**

---

*See HFL's *Secrets of Advanced Bodybuilders, Supplement #1.*

OVERTRAINING AND THE YEAR-ROUND SCHEDULE

Plyometric training sometimes doesn't seem very hard. Nonetheless, it places great stress on the body. Training too often or too much may lead to overtraining syndrome, leaving you tired, listless, and wondering why you're not making any progress.

There are several things you can do to decrease the risk of overtraining. First, when you initially include plyometric exercise as part of your overall training, ease back on other training or lifting until you have adapted to this increased load—for weightlifting, for example, cut back by one set per exercise for the first month. Soon you'll have the explosive strength and power to do even more work!

Second, allow enough rest time between training sessions and stick closely to the recommendation made in **Secrets of Advanced Bodybuilders** to skip a full training session or two once per month.

Third, if you use plyometric training year-round you should employ cycles that vary volume and intensity during the year. A full discussion of cycling—officially known as **periodization**—is beyond the scope of this course. But in lieu of one, we recommend the simple approach of setting aside a month or two each year in which you don't do any plyometrics.

When you have progressed through all levels of the program, you should be well on the way to developing explosive power. Experiment with developing additional plyometric drills for yourself. Many exercises can be done plyometrically to address your specific athletic needs. Just follow the guidelines listed in the last three chapters. And always remember—a little plyo goes a long way.

Until next time, happy training!

❖   ❖   ❖

APPENDIX

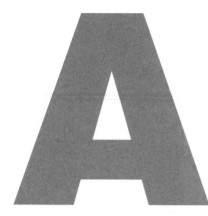

APPENDIX A

DETERMINING YOUR VOLUNTARY ACTIVATION CAPACITY

To calculate your voluntary activation capacity, you need to determine your concentric and eccentric maximums. The procedures to do this are simple. But because you will be dealing with maximum loads—the greatest amount of weight you can handle for one rep—this sort of testing carries a much greater risk of injury than conventional weightlifting.

Please follow the instructions carefully when trying either procedure. There is no way to eliminate the risk of injury during this kind of testing, but following these instructions at least minimizes that risk.

The Basic Procedure

Pick lifts that target the major muscle groups used in your sport. Your safest choices are exercises that allow your body to be well-supported and that don't put a lot of stress on your lower back. For instance, you might use:

■ Bench Press for the pectorals

■ Lat Pull-Downs for the lats

■ Preacher-Bench Curls for the biceps

■ Triceps Press-Downs for the triceps

■ Leg Press for the glutes and quads

■ Leg Curls for the hamstrings

Leg Extensions are not a good choice for testing the quadriceps because of the high shearing forces on the knees during that move.

Determine the concentric and eccentric maximums for these lifts. Don't worry about trying to calculate values for *all* muscle groups or about being painstakingly accurate in measuring your maxes. You're after a general sense of your voluntary activation capacity—basically low (less than 50%) or basically high (greater than 70%). This one's like horseshoes—close is good enough.

Your concentric maximum is simply your one-rep max for a particular lift. After selecting the exercises for which you want to test, follow these steps for each:

(We'll illustrate using the Bench Press.)

■ Find two people you trust to help you with the tests.

■ Warm up *thoroughly* according to the instructions on pages 67 and 68. Before max testing is not the time to cut corners on the warmup.

■ Put the bar on the bench with *no weight on it*. Do about 15 reps slowly and smoothly to get your body "in the groove" for the exercise.

■ Increase the weight to approximately 50% of what you imagine your max to be and do one set of six to eight reps. Rest two minutes.

■ Increase the weight to 70% of your max and do one set of six to eight reps. Rest five full minutes.

■ Increase the weight to what you think is your one-rep max and attempt to do one rep *with your spotters standing by to help if you get into trouble*. If you get a sense that you can't lift the amount you've chosen, *stop trying* and have your spotters lift the weight back onto the rack. This isn't a workout—it's a test. So don't waste energy on lifts you can't do.

■ If you succeeded in performing one rep and you felt as if you might have been able to lift more, rest for five minutes, then increase the weight and repeat the previous step. If you didn't succeed, rest for five minutes, then decrease the weight and try again.

■ If you have to repeat the test more than two or three times, you will probably have to try again on another

Determining Your Concentric Maximum

day because, beyond that point, cummulative fatigue will make it difficult to determine your true concentric max.

Determining Your Eccentric Maximum

Follow the steps below to determine all your eccentric maxes. Once again, we'll use the Bench Press to illustrate.

- Find two people you trust to help you with the tests.
- Warm up *thoroughly* according to the instructions on pages 67 and 68. Again, before max testing is not the time to skimp on the warm-up.
- Put the bar on the bench with *no weight on it*. Do about 15 reps slowly and smoothly to get your body "in the groove" for the exercise.
- Increase the weight to approximately 50% of your max and do one set of six to eight reps. Rest two minutes.
- Increase the weight to 70% of your max and do one set of six to eight reps. Rest five full minutes.
- Increase the weight to an amount equal to your one-rep max plus about 5%. For example, if you're one-rep max is 185 lbs, then increase the weight to about 185 lbs + 5%, or 195 lbs.
- Extend your arms as if you had just finished one rep. Have the spotters lift the bar onto your hands, then attempt to lower the bar under control. Again, the spotters should stay right with you in case you can't control the bar's descent.
- If you succeed in lowering the bar in a controlled manner, increase the weight by another 5% and try again, repeating this procedure until you find the weight at which you can't lower the bar under control. That weight is your eccentric max for this exercise. **Warning: When you find your eccentric max, by definition you won't be able to control the descent of the bar. Your spotters have to be ready to catch it or you could be *severly injured!***
- If you don't succeed in lowering the bar under control, lower the weight by 5% and try again.

■ If you have to repeat the test more than two or three times, you will probably have to try again on another day because cummulative fatigue will make it difficult to determine your true eccentric max.

Doing the Math

Once you have your eccentric and concentric maxes for the different exercises, calculate your voluntary activation capacities by expressing your concentric max as a percentage of your eccentric max.

For instance, if your concentric max for a knee extension is 150 lbs and your eccentric max is 200 lbs, this shows that you can voluntarily lift (150 lbs ÷ 200 lbs) × 100%, or 75% of your absolute maximum—a voluntary activation capacity, then, of 75%.

❖   ❖   ❖

GLOSSARY

Absolute Strength: The total contractile capacity of a muscle; the total tension that would result were all a muscle's fibers to fire in response to maximum stimulation by the nervous system.

Adaptation: The process by which the body increases its ability to handle a greater level of stress or overload.

Anticipatory Contraction: The slight pre-tensing of a muscle prior to contact with the ground or an object. Also known as kinesthetic anticipation, this pre-tensing lets the muscle convert force more efficiently, leading to a more powerful contraction.

Concentric Contraction: A muscle contraction in which the muscle shortens and its corresponding joint angle changes. This is what most people picture when they hear the words *muscle contraction*.

Eccentric Contraction: A muscle contraction where the muscle lengthens as it contracts and the associated joint angle widens.

Eccentric Maximum: The maximum amount of weight that a muscle can resist in an eccentric contraction. The eccentric max tends to be about 40% to 50% greater than your maximum strength, very nearly approximating your absolute strength.

Explosive Strength: The measure of your ability to reach maximum force output in the least time. (See Speed-Strength)

Exercise Sequence: The order in which you do the exercises in your training routine. Proper sequencing is crucial to reaping all the benefits of HFL's synergistic training programs.

Functional Strength Exercises: Exercises that most closely duplicate movements in sports or in everyday life.

Hypertrophy: An increase in overall muscle mass. Bodybuilding focuses on the hypertrophy of muscle.

Intrafusal Fibers: Special muscle fibers within the muscle spindle that are wrapped with nerve cells which relay information from the muscle to the central nervous system. These fibers do not have the contractile capacity of other types of muscle fibers.

Isometric Contraction: A muscle contraction in which both muscle length and joint angle remain unchanged.

Maximum Strength: The greatest amount of force you can generate voluntarily. It is always less than your absolute strength.

Muscle Elasticity: The abililty of muscle to stretch, store, and release energy as the result of imposed tension.

Muscle Spindle: A complex construction of muscle protein, fluid, and nervous system receptors within muscle tissue.

Myotatic Reflex: See *Stretch Reflex*

Overspeed Training: The basis of speed plyometric exercise. Overspeed training creates overload by shortening the period of time in which a movement is normally performed.

Plyometric Training: A method of training for explosive power and speed-strength. Capitalizes on the stretch, or myotatic, reflex to train the voluntary capacity to produce maximum muscle contractions.

Plyotonic Training: A synergistic method of training that combines plyometric exercise with isotonic weightlifting to produce greater explosive power and muscle mass.

Power Endurance: The ability to muster maximum, or near maximum, power repeatedly over time.

Power Endurance Plyometrics: Exercises that develop your ability to sustain maximum power output over time.

Power Plyometrics: Exercises that focus on building explosive strength. They are especially beneficial for sports requiring effort against resistance.

Progressive Overload: Forcing muscles to work harder than they are accustomed over a period of time. As muscles adapt to a given overload, they become capable of doing even more work, and the overload must continuously increase in order to build muscular strength and size.

Rhythm Plyometrics: Plyometric exercises that develop basic strength and coordination through simple drills emphasizing easy, flowing movement. These drills often incorporate a single element of a more difficult and complex movement.

Speed Plyometrics: Plyometric exercises where the overload principle is fulfilled by shortening the time frame in which the exercise takes place. As a consequence, your neuro-muscular system learns to respond more rapidly to stimuli.

Speed-Strength: A measure of strength in relation to time. It describes how long it takes you to produce a given amount of force.

Strength Deficit: The difference between voluntary muscle capacity and absolute capacity. Your strength deficit is also measured by the difference between your maximum eccentric strength and your concentric maximum.

Stretch Reflex: A protective neuro-muscular reaction that triggers a powerful contraction in response to rapid stretching or loading of the muscle. Tension in the intrafusal muscle fibers stimulates nerve cells, sending messages out to the central nervous system at great speed. In response, the central nervous system triggers a muscle reflex that generates a fast and powerful contraction. Also known as the myotatic reflex.

Starting Strength: The measure of your ability to generate force at the start of an action.

Synergism: Combining elements to create a whole greater than just the sum of those elements.

Training Duration: The length of time you train in a given workout. Also measured by the number of contacts or repetitions.

Training Frequency: The number of times you train within a given time frame.

Training Intensity: The degree of exertion, or how hard you force yourself to work. In weight training, intensity is measured as a percentage of maximum strength performed within a given time frame.

Training Mode: The type of exercise(s) that comprise your training program.

Voluntary Activation Capacity: The percentage of your absolute strength you can actually use.

❖　　❖　　❖

BIBLIOGRAPHY

TEXT SOURCES

Bosco, C. / Komi, P.V., "Muscle Elasticity in Athletes," in P. Komi (ed), *Exercise and Sport Biology*, Human Kinetics Publishers, 1982.

Chu, D.A., *Jumping Into Plyometrics*, Leisure Press, Champaign, IL, 1992.

Costello, Frank, *Bounding to the Top: The Complete Book on Plyometrics and Training for All Sports*, Athletic Training Consultants, Inc., West Bowie, MD, 1984.

Davis, J., *Plyometrics and Related Topics: A Selected Bibliography*, Australian Sports Commission, National Sport Information Center Canberra, 1992.

Freeman, Will / Freeman, Evelyn, *Plyometrics: Complete Training for All Sports*, Championship Books, Ames, IA, 1984.

Jacoby, E. / Gambetta, V., "Strength Development," in Gambetta, V., (ed) *The Athletics Congress's Track and Field Coaching Manual* —Second Edition, Leisure Press, Champiagn, IL, 1989.

Matveyev, L., *Fundamentals of Sports Training*, Progress Publishers, Moscow, 1972.

O'Connell / Gardner, E., *Understanding the Scientific Basis of Human Movement*, Williams and Wilkins, Baltimore, MD, 1972.

Radcliffe, James A. / Farentinos, Robert C., *Plyometrics: Explosive Power Training*, Human Kinetics Publishers, Champaign, IL, 1985.

Stolley, S. / Derse, E. (eds), "Plyometric Training for Speed-Strength in Track and Field," *Track and Field Coaches Manual*, Amateur Athletic Foundation of Los Angeles, 1992.

Wilt, F., "Plyometrics: What It Is and How It Works," in Allsen, P.E. (ed), *Conditioning and Physical Fitness: Current Answers to Relevant Questions*, Brown, Dubuque, IA, 1978.

Yessis, Michael / Hatfiled, Frederick C., *Plyometric Training: Achieving Power and Explosiveness in Sports*, Fitness Systems, Canoga Park, CA, 1986.

VIDEO SOURCES

Brittenham, D. / Brittenham, G., *Leap to the Top: Applying Plyometrics* (videorecording), National Institute for Fitness and Sport, North Palm Beach, FL, 1990.

Gambetta, Vern / Cloidt, Susan, *Methods in Plyometric Training* (videorecording), National Strength and Conditioning Association, Lincoln, NB, 1989.

Bezer, Gregory A./ Radcliffe, James A., *Plyometrics: Explosive Power Training for Every Sport* (videorecording), Human Kinetics Videos, Champaign, IL, 1985.

Myers, Bob, *Plyometrics* (videorecording), Truckee River Studios, Alamo, CA, 1982 (1990 reprint).

JOURNAL SOURCES

Adams, T.; "An Investigation of Selected Plyometric Training Exercises on Muscular Leg Strength and Power," *Track and Field Quarterly Review*. 84(1):36-40.

Aura, O. & Komi, P.V.; "Effects of Prestretch Intensity on Mechanical Efficiency of Positive Work on Elastic Behavior of Skeletal Muscle in Stretch-Shortening Cycle Exercises," *International Journal of Sports Medicine*. 1986; 7:137-143.

Bauer, T., Thayer, R.E. & Baras, G.; "Comparison of Training Modalities for Power Development in the Lower Extremity," *Journal of Applied Sport Science Research*. Oct-Nov, 1990; 4(4).

Bielek, E., et al.; "Roundtable: Practical Considerations for Utilizing Plyometrics, Part 1," *National Strength and Conditioning Association Journal*. Jun-Jul, 1986; 8(3):14-22.

Bielek, E., et al.; "Roundtable: Practical Considerations for Utilizing Plyometrics, Part 2," *National Strength and Conditioning Association Journal*. Aug-Sept, 1986; 8(4):14-24.

Blakely, J.B. & Southard, D.; "The Combined Effects of Weight Training and Plyometrics on Dynamic Leg Strength and Power," *Journal of Applied Sport Research*. Feb-Mar, 1987; 1(1):14-16.

Bosco, C., et al.; "Prestretch Potentiation of Human Skeletal Muscle During Ballistic Movement," *Acta Physiologica Scandinavica*. 1981; 11:135-140.

Brzycki, M.; "Plyometrics: A Giant Step Backwards," *Athletic Journal*. Apr, 1986; 66(9):22-23.

Brzycki, M.; "Point: Plyometrics Are Unsafe," *Coaching Volleyball*. Jun-Jul, 1988; 1(5).

Chu, D.A. & Plummer, L.; "The Language of Plyometrics," *National Strength and Conditioning Association Journal*. Oct-Nov, 1984; 6(5):30-31.

Clutch, D., et al.; "Effect of Depth Jumps and Weight Training on Leg Strength and Vertical Jump," *Research Quarterly for Exercise and Sport*. Mar, 1983; 54(1):5-10.

Costello, F.; "Using Weight Training and Plyometrics to Increase Explosive Power for Football," *National Strength and Conditioning Association Journal*. Apr-May, 1984; 6(2):22- 25.

DeSpain, R. & Chevrette, J.M.; "Plyometrics in Athletics," *Journal of Applied Research in Coaching and Athletics*. 1987; 2(3):185-197.

DiBrezzo, R., et al.; "The Effects of a Modified Plyometric Program on Junior High Female Basketball Players," *Journal of Applied Research in Coaching and Athletics*. 1988; 3(3):172-181.

Dick, F.; "Development of Maximum Sprint Speed," *Track Technique*. Fall, 1989; (109):3478-86.

Duda, M.; "Plyometrics: A Legitimate Form of Power Training," *Physician and Sportsmedicine*. Mar, 1988; 16(3):212-216.

Duke, S. & BenEliyahu, D.; "Plyometrics: Optimizing Athletic Performance Through the Development of Power as Assessed by Vertical Leap Ability—An Observational Study," *Chiropractic Sports Medicine*. Feb, 1992; 6(1):10-15.

Ford, H.T., et al.; "Effects of Three Combinations of Plyometric and Weight Training Programs on Selected Physical Fitness Test Items," *Perceptual and Motor Skills*. Jun, 1983; 56(3):919-922.

Gambetta, V.; "Plyometrics for Beginners: Basic Considerations," *New Studies in Athletics*. Mar, 1989; 4(1):61-66.

Goss, K.; "Counterpoint: Correctly Used, Plyometrics are Safe," *Coaching Volleyball*. Jun-Jul, 1988; 1(5).

Graves, J.E., et.al.; "Effects of Reduced Training Frequency on Muscular Strength," *International Journal of Sports Medicine*. 1988; 9:316-319.

Hennessy, L.; "Plyometrics: Important Technical Considerations," *Athletics Coach*. Dec, 1990; 24(4):18-21.

Hiserman, Jim; "Plyometrics for Jumpers," *American Athletics*. Spring, 1993; 5(1).

Horrigan, J. & Shaw, D.; "Think Before You Leap," *Track and Field Quarterly Review*. Winter, 1989; 89(4):41-43.

Javorek, I.; "Plyometrics," *National Strength and Conditioning Association Journal*. Apr-May, 1989; 11(2):52-57.

Koutedakis, Y.; "Muscle Elasticity—Plyometrics: Some Physiological and Practical Considerations," *Journal of Applied Research in Coaching and Athletics*. 1989; 4(1):35-49.

Lundin, P.; "A Review of Plyometric Training," *National Strength and Conditioning Association Journal*. Jun-Jul, 1985; 7(3):69-74.

Lundin, P.; "Plyometric Training Loads for Youths and Beginners," *Track Technique*. Fall, 1987; (101):3211-3213.

Lundin, P.; "A Review of Plyometric Training," *Track and Field Quarterly Review*. Winter, 1989; 89(4):37-40.

Mann, R.; "Plyometrics," *Track and Field Quarterly Review*. Winter 1981; 81(4):55-57.

Mann, R.; "The Biomechanical Analysis of Sprinters," *Track Technique*. Winter, 1986; (94):3000-3003.

Paish, Wilf; "The Development of Strength and Power," *New Studies in Athletics*. 1992; 7:2, 45-54.

Pauletto, B.; "Basics of Plyometric Training," *American Fitness Quarterly*. Oct, 1987; 6:38-40.

Reiff, M.A.; "Hydroplys: A Safe Efficient Plyometric Workout," *Track and Field Quarterly Review*. Winter, 1988; 88(4).

Santos, J.; "Increasing Throwing Speed through Upper Body Plyometrics," *Track and Field Quarterly Review*. Fall, 1987; 87(3):29-33.

Smythe, R.; "Using Plyometrics in Systematic Conditioning," *Coaching Clinic*. Sept, 1991; 30(1):6-7.

Smythe, R.; "Plyometrics: Before You Jump In," *Texas Coach.* Nov, 1991; 36(4):52-53.

Thomas, D.W.; "Plyometrics: More Than the Stretch Reflex," *National Strength and Conditioning Association Journal.* Oct-Nov, 1988; 10(5):49-51.

Tidow, Gunter; "Aspects of Strength Training in Athletics," *New Studies in Athletics.* 1990; 1:93-110.

Verkhoshanski, T.; "Depth Jumping in the Training of Jumpers," *Track Technique.* 1973; (41):1618-1619.

Verkoshanski, T.; "Perspectives in the Improvement of Speed-Strength Preparation of Jumpers," *Yessis Review of Soviet Sports.* 1969; 4(2):28-29.

Verkoshanksi, T. & Tatyan, V.; "Speed-Strength Preparation of Future Champions," *Soviet Sports Review.* 1983; 18(4):166-170

VonDuvillard, S., et al.; "Plyometrics for Speed and Explosiveness," *Scholastic Coach.* Mar, 1990; 59(8):80-81.

Wajciechowski, J.; "Plyometrics: Is It Right for Everyone?," *Aerobics and Fitness.* Jan-Feb, 1987; 5(1):42-43.

Wilgren, S.; "The Plyometrics Debate: Safe and Beneficial or Dangerous and Unproven?," *Coaching Volleyball.* Jun-Jul, 1988; 1(5):8-12.

Wilson, G.J., et al.; "The Use of Elastic Energy in Sport," *Sports Coach.* Jul-Sept, 1990; 13(3):8-10.

Wilt, F.; "Plyometrics: What It Is, and How It Works," *Athletic Journal.* May, 1975; 55(9).

Wilt, F.; "Plyometrics," *Track Technique.* Mar, 1976; (63).

Yessis, M.; "Speed/Explosiveness with Plyometrics," *Scholastic Coach.* Feb, 1991; 60(7).

INDEX

Legendary Abs II

Featuring the Synergism principle, **Legendary Abs II** guarantees rock-hard, well-defined abdominals in just 6 minutes a day! See results within two weeks, or your money back. Not isometrics or some other supposed shortcut, Legendary Abs II is just good science applied to bodybuilding. Over 350,000 copies sold worldwide! *A 48 p. illustrated manual.*

SynerAbs II: 6 Minutes to a Flatter Stomach

Women's edition of the **Legendary Abs II** program. Guarantees a firm, well-toned midsection in just 6 minutes a day! Ten levels of routines from beginning to advanced. *A 48 p. illustrated manual.*

Beyond Legendary Abs: A Synergistic Guide to *Legendary Abs II* and *SynerAbs II*

We know the serious bodybuilder is always reaching for greater gains. In letter after letter, our readers unanimously ask, "How can I go *further*?" The answer is in **Beyond Legendary Abs**—a new performance guide specially designed to supplement our phenomenally successful **Legendary Abs II** and **SynerAbs II** programs. It's the closest thing we can offer to a personal trainer! **Beyond** is not just for advanced bodybuilders! It's just as useful for the **beginner** trying to get the most out of the program, or the **intermediate** on level 5 trying to break through a plateau. It's a detailed performance guide designed to maximize the efficiency of your training **at any level.** Now is the time to go *beyond! A 24 p. illustrated manual.*

Secrets of Advanced Bodybuilders

What **Legendary Abs** and **SynerAbs** do for abdominal conditioning, **Secrets of Advanced Bodybuilders** does for your whole workout! **Secrets** explains how to apply the Synergism principle to training back, chest, delts, biceps, triceps, quads, and hamstrings. It unlocks the secrets of the Optimum Workout, and shows you how to develop the best routines for *you*—with your particular goals, strengths, and body structure.

Get the *ultimate* program. Plus, learn... ❏ a new back exercise that will pile on the mass and increase power without putting harmful stress on your lower back ❏ a technique for making Leg Extensions 200% more intense by targeting both inner *and outer* quads ❏ the shift in position that cranks Pull-Up and Pull-Down exercises to 3 times normal intensity ❏ a *body weight* triceps exercise that will be "a growing experience" even for someone who's been training for years ❏ a *body weight* lat exercise that will mass up your back faster than you would have believed possible ❏ a special shoulder set that's more effective than most entire delt routines—also—❏ the best way to integrate your other athletic endeavors—running, cycling, stretching, mountain climbing, martial arts, etc.—into your routine to create the optimum overall program ❏ techniques for maximizing the effectiveness of *all* exercises you do, not just those in the course...and much, much more! *Stop working harder than you need to to get the results you want. 158 pp. Over 300 illustrations.* **Now available on video, too!**

Secrets of Advanced Bodybuilders, Supplement #1

New breakthroughs in sports research are happening all the time. With the **Secrets** course as its foundation, the SUPPLEMENT series provides the most complete and up-to-date training resource available. Supplement #1 features a new 5-day split based on a unique three-week cycle that reduces workout time and minimizes the risk of overtraining. You'll also learn: ❏ optimum use of the jettison and pyramiding techniques (when these are effective, when not, how they fit into the **Secrets** routines) ❏ altering rep and set numbers to affect tendon or muscular strength, local muscular endurance, or speed ❏ machines vs. free weights and the best way to use both ❏ Exercise SetPoint, a brand-new concept integral to getting maximum results in minimum time. *All this, and a lot more! A 24 p. illustrated manual.*

SynerStretch: For Total Body Flexibility...FAST!

Two programs in one: Both deliver lower- and upper-body flexibility in less than 8 minutes a day! **Syner-Stretch A** is for you if you need to maintain your flexibility. Originally designed for martial artists—who depend on extreme flexibility— **SynerStretch A** will also help bodybuilders, dancers, and other athletes stay flexible in less than *5 minutes per workout.* A great way to end a training session of any kind! **SynerStretch B** is for you if you need to increase your flexibility. Not only does it take less than 8 minutes, but because it makes use of a new, relatively unknown technique (Isometric Agonist Contraction/Relaxation), it eliminates most of the pain usually associated with stretching. It works! When you order **SynerStretch**, you get both programs in one manual. *Get loose, and stay loose with **SynerStretch**. A 28 p. illustrated manual.* **Also available on video.**

Power ForeArms!

Here at last is a program that specifically targets the hard-to-develop forearm muscles. Like all Health For Life programs, **Power ForeArms!** is based on the Synergism principle and yields maximum results in minimum time. Designed for serious bodybuilders and martial artists, **Power ForeArms!** will help you build strong, solid, massive forearms in just 7 to 12 minutes, twice a week. Give **Power ForeArms!** a try. *A 32 p. illustrated manual.* **Also available on video.**

SynerShape: A Scientific Weight Loss Guide

We're surrounded by weight loss myths. Crash diets. Spot reducing. Exotic herbs. Still, most plans fail, and most people who lose weight gain it back again. Is there really an honest, effective solution? **Yes! Syner-Shape** represents the next generation in awareness of how the body gains and metabolizes fat. It synthesizes the most recent findings on nutrition, exercise, and psychology into a TOTAL program, offering you the tools you need to shape the body you want. **SynerShape** works. Let it work for *you! A 24 p. illustrated manual.*

The Psychology of Weight Loss

This special program-on-tape picks up where **SynerShape** leaves off. Noted psychologist Carol Landesman explores eating problems and *solutions* based on the latest research into human behavior and metabolism. Then, through a series of exercises, she helps you begin to heal the emotional conflicts behind your weight problem. **The Psychology of Weight Loss** is a unique program that brings the power of the therapy process into the privacy of your home. *A 90-minute guided introspection. On audio cassette.*

The 7-Minute Rotator Cuff Solution

Almost everyone who works out experiences some kind of rotator cuff injury during a lifetime of training. Any of these injuries could spell the end of a workout career, but most can be prevented. **The 7-Minute Rotator Cuff Solution** is a quick, simple program to help prevent (or help you recover from) rotator cuff injuries. It details how the shoulder works, what can go wrong and why, and exactly what to do (and not do) to stop shoulder problems before they happen. Plus: a simple 7-minute exercise program that can eliminate shoulder pain and restore normal shoulder function in just a few weeks. *144 pp., illustrated.*

For price and order information, or
to receive a FREE copy of the Health For Life Catalogue
call 1-800-874-5339
or write us at...

Health For Life
Suite 483, 8033 Sunset Blvd.
Los Angeles, CA 90046-2427

Notes